The Government Manager's Guide to Plain Language

Judith Gillespie Myers, PhD

MANAGEMENTCONCEPTS PRESS

MANAGEMENTCONCEPTS PRESS
8230 Leesburg Pike, Suite 800
Tysons Corner, VA 22182
(703) 790-9595
Fax: (703) 790-1371
www.managementconcepts.com

Printed in the United States of America

Library of Congress Control Number: 2013933787

ISBN 978-1-56726-422-7

ABOUT THE AUTHOR

Judith Gillespie Myers, Ph.D., is an instructor and writer who has taught writing skills to hundreds of government employees. Her publications include *Essentials of School Management, Banishing Bureaucratese: Using Plain Language in Government Writing, Plain Language in Government Writing: A Step-by-Step Guide, How to Select and Use Learning Tools*, and *Enhance Learning Retention*, as well as numerous articles and more than 20 training manuals. As a journalist, radio newscaster, and news editor, Dr. Myers has written numerous articles and news items. She received her doctorate from American University in Washington, D.C.

The Government Manager's Guide to Plain Language

The Government Manager's Essential Library

The Government Manager's Essential Library is a series of easy-to-use, subject-specific guides on issues every government manager faces:

1. *The Government Manager's Guide to Appropriations Law,* William G. Arnold, CDFM-A
2. *The Government Manager's Guide to Source Selection,* Charles D. Solloway, Jr., CPCM
3. *The Government Manager's Guide to Contract Negotiation,* LeGette McIntyre
4. **The Government Manager's Guide to Plain Language, Judith Gillespie Myers, Ph.D.**
5. *The Government Manager's Guide to the Work Breakdown Structure,* Gregory T. Haugan, Ph.D., PMP
6. *The Government Manager's Guide to Strategic Planning,* Kathleen E. Monahan
7. *The Government Manager's Guide to Project Management,* Jonathan Weinstein, PMP, and Timothy Jaques, PMP
8. *The Government Manager's Guide to Leading Teams,* Lisa DiTullio
9. *The Government Manager's Guide to Earned Value Management,* Charles I. Budd, PMP, and Charlene S. Budd, Ph.D., CPA, CMA, CFM, PMP
10. *The Government Manager's Guide to the Statement of Work,* Michael G. Martin, PMP
11. *The Government Manager's Guide to Contract Law,* Terrence O'Connor

To my husband, Geof

CONTENTS

PREFACE

One of the most common requirements in any job posting is excellent communication skills. This is especially true for managers, in both the government and the private sector. Managers need to write clearly, concisely, and in a manner that appeals to a wide audience. They must make instructions and policies clear to employees; give effective presentations; deliver useful, fair performance appraisals; write persuasive budget justifications; negotiate with both staff and management at all levels; and explain clearly to the public how to obtain benefits or comply with requirements.

Traditionally, government documents were written in legalistic, confusing language. Too often, this style resulted in reader frustration, lawsuits, and lack of trust between citizens and their government.

Today, those in both government and industry are appreciating the value of plain, understandable English. The passage of the Plain Language Act of 2010 demonstrated a commitment to clearer communication. Despite a simple-looking outcome, however, plain language is hard work. It requires a clear vision of the purpose of the document, an understanding of the audience, and a willingness to strive for the most uncluttered, direct message possible.

The purpose of this book is to make this process easier and more understandable. *The Government Manager's Guide to Plain Language* is based on the 2008 book *Plain Language in Government Writing: A Step-by-Step Guide*; that book has been condensed and focused more directly on the needs of managers. We have added sections on statements of work, position descriptions, performance appraisals, Exhibit 300 reports, and talking points, as well as a chapter on social media. We have also inserted relevant tips for government managers in each chapter.

Although the guidelines presented in this book will help with any kind of writing, the main focus of the book is on government workplace writing. Government managers need to understand and be able to apply the principles and mechanics of plain language, and they must model clear, effective writing for their staffs. The ability to write well correlates highly with the ability to think well—to analyze information, weigh alternatives, and make decisions. Communicating clearly is as essential an element in career success in the government as it is in a corporate environment.

Because writing is the process of getting thoughts onto paper, clear writing helps the writer develop, focus, and organize ideas. It helps writers understand their thoughts better. Managers who can organize their thoughts, write them clearly, and present them effectively are well on their way to success in the government workplace.

—Judith Gillespie Myers

ACKNOWLEDGMENTS

I would like to thank everyone on the Management Concepts team who made this publication possible, especially Myra Strauss, for her fine editing, encouragement, and guidance. Also, a special thanks to Shelley Kais for her suggestions and support.

Chapter 1

SUCCEEDING AS A WRITER IN TODAY'S GOVERNMENT WORKPLACE

To succeed in the government workplace, you must be able to express yourself effectively, clearly, and persuasively. You must create documents that your readers will read and understand, that result in decisions, and that affect your readers as you intend. Each letter, report, or email you send out is a reflection of your agency or department. It is also a reflection of you personally.

Many of us find the whole process of writing daunting. Yet, with the right guidance and practice, we can all become better, more effective writers.

THE IMPORTANCE OF PLAIN LANGUAGE IN GOVERNMENT WRITING

Government writing presents a special challenge. Government documents often contain technical information, and they go out to multiple audiences—some highly knowledgeable, some less so.

Government documents have traditionally contained gobbledygook or "bureaucratese"—jargon and complicated, legalistic language. These uninviting letters and reports read as though they are addressed to technical experts and lawyers rather than to readers who need to be influenced or informed. However, a few small changes can turn these documents into clear, effective messages.

Presidential Efforts to Improve Government Writing

For decades, presidents and political leaders have urged clear writing in government documents. James Madison wrote in 1788, "It will be of little avail to the people, that the laws are made by men of their own choice, if the laws be so voluminous that they cannot be read, or so incoherent that they cannot be understood."[1]

Franklin Roosevelt cringed at the convoluted wording of the following blackout order during World War II:

> *Such preparations shall be made as will completely obscure all Federal buildings and non-Federal buildings occupied by the government during an air raid for any period of time from visibility by reason of internal or external illumination.*

"Tell them," Roosevelt said, "that in buildings where they have to keep the work going to put something across the windows."[2]

In an attempt to cut the government gobbledygook, President Nixon ordered that the *Federal Register* be written in "layman's terms." President Carter signed an executive order directing that federal regulations be "easy to understand by those who are required to comply with them." A few federal agencies responded by publishing regulations that were more clearly written, although the efforts were sporadic.

The Clinton administration issued monthly "No Gobbledygook Awards" to agencies that cut the bureaucratese. In 1998, President Clinton issued a directive requiring government agencies to use plain English. Several agencies set up what is now called PLAIN—the Plain Language Action and Information Network, a governmentwide group to improve communications from the federal government to the public.[3] The PLAIN website (www.plainlanguage.gov) offers numerous resources to help writers communicate more clearly.

The Plain Writing Act of 2010

Plain language in government writing became the law when President Obama passed the Plain Writing Act of 2010. The law defines plain writing as writing that is "clear, concise, well-organized, and follows other best practices appropriate to the subject or field and intended audience."

This law requires each agency to use plain writing in every covered document the agency issues or substantially revises. A "covered document" is any document that meets one of the following criteria:

- Is necessary for obtaining any federal benefit or service or filing taxes
- Provides information about any federal benefit or service
- Explains to the public how to comply with a requirement the federal government administers or enforces.

Covered documents include (whether in paper or electronic form) letters, publications, forms, notices, and instructions, but not regulations.

In addition, the Plain Language Act requires that each agency take the following steps:

1. Designate one or more senior officials within the agency to oversee the agency's implementation of the act.
2. Communicate the act's requirements to the agency's employees.
3. Train agency employees in "plain writing" (defined as writing that is clear, concise, well-organized, and follows other best practices appropriate to the subject or field and intended audience).
4. Establish a process for overseeing the agency's ongoing compliance with the act's requirements.
5. Create and maintain a plain writing section of the agency's website to inform the public of agency compliance with the requirements of the act, provide a mechanism for the agency to receive and respond to public input on agency implementation and agency reports required under the act, and be accessible from its homepage.
6. Designate one or more agency points-of-contact to receive and respond to public input on the implementation of the act.[4]

Other Plain Language Programs

Efforts to eliminate bureaucratese have not only come from the White House. Many federal agencies, state government entities, and other organizations have initiated programs to enforce plain language:

- The Center for Medicare and Medicaid Services offers a *Toolkit for Making Written Material Clear and Effective*. Its focus is health-related materials, but it can be used for many other topics.
- U.S. Citizenship and Immigration Services has a thriving plain-language program and provides training for its staff throughout the country. As part of that program, it developed a series of short, funny videos highlighting different plain-language techniques.
- The Federal Aviation Administration established FAA writing standards in March 2003 and posted the FAA's *Plain Language Manual*
- The *Federal Register* offers several resources online, including guidance on how to make regulations readable, how to draft a legal document, and how to rewrite a short rule.
- The Securities and Exchange Commission provides *A Plain English Handbook: How to Create Clear SEC Disclosure Documents* online.

- The Department of the Army, the National Institutes of Health, and the Centers for Disease Control have all developed training available for anyone to use.

Many states and municipalities also have laws requiring that consumer statutes be written in plain language:

- The Washington State Government has been involved in the plain language movement since the mid–1990s. In 2005, the governor issued an executive order requiring all state agencies to use simple and clear language when communicating with citizens and businesses.
- Texas has a plain language contracts project, including a plain language submission form for contracts.
- The Mayor's Office of Adult Education in New York City provides *Easy to Read NYC: Guidelines for Clear and Effective Communication*.

The Federal Judicial Center in Washington, D.C., teaches federal judges to write their opinions in plain English. The American Bar Association has issued a resolution encouraging agencies to write regulations in plain language.[5]

WHY USE PLAIN LANGUAGE?

Proponents assert that writing documents using plain language techniques is effective in a number of ways: It saves money, helps prevent lawsuits, engages readers, and makes you more successful.

Plain Language Saves Money

A 1991 study showed that writing memos in plain language instead of bureaucratese could save the U.S. Navy $250–$350 million a year. Naval officers were given business memos to read. Some memos were written in plain style and some in bureaucratic style. It took officers 17–23 percent less time to read a plain memo. Based on the average hourly pay for all naval personnel, the researchers calculated the yearly savings.[6]

As part of a writing project, the Veterans Administration tracked the savings from rewriting just one form letter in plain language. In one year, a regional VA call center saw the number of calls drop from about 1,100 to about 200. A VA project coordinator estimated that, if this letter alone were adopted at VA offices nationwide, the VA would save more than $40,000 a year. Of course, the VA sends out thousands of different letters each year.[7]

Agencies have been cutting down on administrative costs, too. In the 1970s the Federal Communications Commission rewrote the regulations for CB radios in plain English. The number of calls from people confused by the rules dropped so dramatically that the agency was able to reassign all five people who had been fielding questions full-time.[8]

Examples of how using fewer words has resulted in reduced time and cost—and greater ease of public use—abound throughout the government. One outstanding example is the Farm Credit Administration, which revised a document explaining the Freedom of Information Act fees. The reduced size of the document—from 7,850 to 4,018 words—made it more user-friendly for the public and lowered the printing cost. Interestingly, the revised document contained more information than the original.[9]

Plain Language Helps Prevent Lawsuits

Unclear writing is more than annoying; some courts have called it unconstitutional. For example:

> *A few years ago, the Immigration and Naturalization Service (INS) was taken to court by several aliens the INS had attempted to deport after they had failed to request hearings in document fraud cases. The INS had notified them of their right to request a hearing and informed them that, if they waived that right, they most likely would be deported.*
>
> *The problem? The forms the INS used for notification were so unclear that the aliens didn't understand their rights or the possible legal consequences. The court not only ordered INS to rewrite the forms but also prevented the agency from deporting any alien who had received the forms.*[10]

Plain Language Engages Readers

Research shows that readers prefer documents written in plain language and understand them better. For example, the research director of the Plain Language Commission in the United Kingdom, used his own guidelines to revise a document and later tested it against the original. The result was that 87 percent of the law students tested preferred the revised document. More important, when asked a set of 12 questions about either the original or the revised document, students using the revised version performed better on nine out of 12 questions.[11]

In a similar study, two separate surveys were sent to judges and lawyers, one written in traditional legalese and the other written in plain English (though they were not labeled as such). The readers rated the passages written in legalese to be substantially weaker and less persuasive than the versions written in plain English.[12]

If people understand your documents the first time they read them, they will be less likely to ask for clarification and more likely to respond favorably to your message.

Plain Language Makes You More Successful

It's difficult these days to find a job that does not list excellent written and verbal communication skills as one of the requirements—especially for a manager. A quick glance at jobs posted on such sites as Monster.com shows that applicants for a variety of management positions all must have this qualification.

The U.S. Office of Personnel Management (OPM) recognizes the need for communication skills among its managers. OPM's Leadership Education and Development Certificate Program includes "Effective Writing in the Federal Government" in three of the five leadership tracks: Project/Team Lead, Supervisor, and Leadership for Professionals. The executive track includes "Executive Communication Skills: Leading the Process of Change." Both the supervisor and the manager tracks list the course "Communicating Face to Face."[13]

A description of Senior Executive Service qualifications states that senior executives "must move beyond using communication skills to represent the organization to using communication for team and partnership building."[14]

> **Manager Alert**
>
> Clear writing can boost your reputation and enhance your government career.

NOTES

1. James Madison, *The Federalist Papers*, no. 62 (New Rochelle, NY: Arlington House, 1966).
2. Cited in William Zinsser, *On Writing Well: The Classic Guide to Writing Nonfiction*, 7th ed. (New York: HarperCollins, 2006), 7.
3. For more information on the history of PLAIN, see "History of Plain Language in the United States." Online at www.plain language.gov (accessed January 2013).
4. www.gpo.gov/fdsys/pkg/PLAW-111publ274/pdf/PLAW-111publ274.pdf (accessed January 2013).
5. Plain Language Action and Information Network, "American Bar Association Adoption by the House of Delegates." Online at www.plainlanguage.gov (accessed January 2013).
6. Joseph Kimble, "Writing for Dollars, Writing to Please," *The Scribes Journal of Legal Writing* 6 (1996).
7. Ibid.
8. Ibid.
9. Archive, National Partnership for Reinventing Government, "Morley Winograd Plain Language Award Presentations," Washington, DC, April 6, 2000. Online at http://govinfo.library.unt.edu/npr/library/speeches/040600.html (accessed January 2013).
10. Mark R. Miller, "Is It Plain English Yet? Bureaucratese Makes People Read Between the Lines," *The Editorial Eye* (March 1999).

11. Martin Cutts, "Unspeakable Acts Revisited," *Information Design Journal* 9, no. 1 (1998): 39–43. Cited in Beth Mazur, "Revisiting Plain Language." Online at www.plainlanguage.gov (accessed January 2013).
12. Joseph Kimble, "Writing for Dollars, Writing to Please," *The Scribes Journal of Legal Writing* 6 (1996).
13. https://leadership.opm.gov/certificates/LEAD/LEAD_Brochure_2012.pdf (accessed January 2013).
14. www.opm.gov/ses/recruitment/qrbprocess.asp (accessed January 2013).

Chapter 2

GETTING STARTED: THE PLANNING STAGE

All of us have times when we just can't seem to face a writing task. Whether starting a long report or a memo, we find ourselves staring at a blank screen, our minds wandering. At those times, the writing process can seem so overwhelming that we'll do anything to avoid putting down that first word.

If you're having a difficult time getting started and think you might be experiencing writer's block, try the following:

- Avoid leaving your project until the last minute.
- When scheduling your project, give yourself some time to warm up to the topic.
- Jot down every idea that comes to you, quickly and randomly.
- If you run into a roadblock after you get started, take a break and let your ideas incubate.
- Don't confuse writing with editing.

Writing proceeds much more easily when writers recognize the phases of the writing process: (1) planning, (2) drafting, and (3) editing. Although you might move back and forth from one stage to another, the important thing to remember is not to combine the stages. Each stage requires a distinctly different process and way of thinking. For example, during the drafting phase, you should not edit. Drafting requires that you allow your thoughts to flow freely. If you try to edit while you draft, you'll inhibit the flow of ideas.

GUIDELINES FOR PLANNING

For any kind of writing—emails, letters, or reports— you need to make sure that you understand your purpose, your audience, and your subject.

Know Your Purpose

Before you begin, ask yourself why you are writing. This will save time for both you and others.

Decide what effect you want to have on your reader. Identify the most important idea—the one you want the reader to remember. A one- or two-sentence purpose statement helps get you started. It becomes the lead-in to your outline and often becomes the first words in the document itself.

The following are examples of purpose statements:

- To persuade the deputy to add three new staff members to the human resources team
- To provide background information on a policy that is coming up for review
- To direct employees to use a new timesheet procedure.

Know Your Audience

Typically, the role (or category) of your reader determines what the reader knows about your subject, the reader's decision-making level, and the type or form of information needed.

To gauge your reader's reaction, ask yourself the following questions:

- Is your message in alignment with your reader's goals and values?
- Are you disputing the data?
- Will your reader lose face by accepting your recommendations?
- Will your message create more work for your reader?
- Will your reader get pressure from his or her manager because of your message?

Once you have answered these questions, you can write your document in a way that minimizes negative reactions.

Writing Regulations for More Than One Reader

A document often has many readers. You might be writing to exporters and importers, coal miners and surface owners, or airlines and passengers.

The following are some tips for writing regulations for diverse audiences[1]:

- Break your document down into the essential elements.
- Determine which elements apply to each part of your audience.
- Group the elements according to the audience that will be affected. For example, if you are writing about research grants for university professors,

first tell the professors what they have to do and then tell the university accounting department what it has to do.

- Clearly identify to whom you are speaking in each section. Don't make a reader go through material only to find out at the end that the section doesn't apply.

Writing Letters and Reports for More Than One Reader

When you are writing a letter or report, you generally write to only one person. However, in many cases there will be many readers. Your entire audience will need to understand your letter or report.

Distinguish between primary readers (such as members of Congress) and secondary readers (such as constituents). *Primary readers* are those who have the greatest need to know. They are the decisionmakers, the ones who will need to act after reading your report. These are the readers to whom you should gear your writing. *Secondary readers* are those who, though interested, do not need the same level of detail.

Know Your Subject

Once you've determined your purpose and identified your audience, you need to research your subject. Collect all the information you need (but don't overdo it):

- Review correspondence, policy directives, and administrative memos or any other papers related to your task.
- Consult with people who can lend knowledge or insight.
- Analyze your notes or your data collection.
- Determine what is useful and what is not.
- Organize useful material into meaningful groups.

Manager Alert

If you are assigning a writing task, make sure the writer is very clear about the purpose and audience, as well as the approximate length and the due date. Also, provide clear guidelines on where and how to collect information from both documents and individuals.

GUIDELINES FOR BRAINSTORMING AND ORGANIZING

Once you've determined your purpose, audience, and subject, think about what you have to say and then organize your thoughts. First, spend some time brainstorming. Let your ideas flow freely, get them down on paper, and then evaluate and organize them. The following are some suggestions for brainstorming or generating ideas.

The Mind Map

Mind mapping uses a nonlinear, pictorial way of presenting ideas and their relationship to each other.[2] To brainstorm in this way, follow these steps:

1. In the center of a large piece of paper, write the most important word or phrase describing your main idea (e.g., a proposal for new software). Circle it.
2. Draw lines radiating outward from that main idea. Each line represents another important concept you want to present (e.g., costs).
3. Along each line, draw smaller lines representing related or supporting ideas (e.g., software).
4. Continue this process, adding in ideas as they occur to you, until you have developed a wheel-like picture (as shown in Figure 2-1) of the ideas you want to cover.
5. Edit your mind map. Think about the relationship of the outside items to the center item. Combine or move ideas for better organization.
6. Organize those ideas into a traditional outline.

FIGURE 2-1
Sample Mind Map

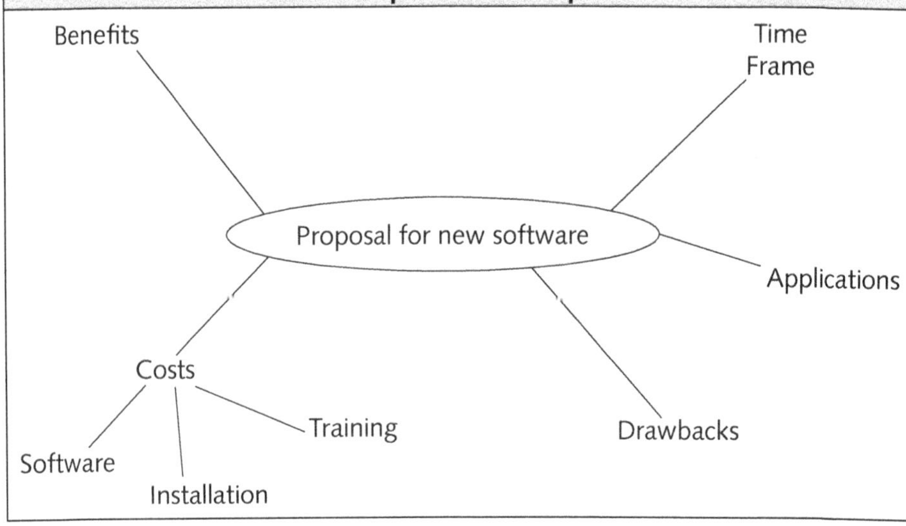

Questioning

Create an imaginary dialogue in which you play two parts: the writer and the reader. List questions the reader will ask, and write your answers underneath. Answer your questions as clearly and completely as possible. Then organize those ideas into a traditional outline.

Index Cards

This tried-and-true term paper technique allows you to rearrange ideas easily. Simply use one card for each item of information you want to cover and then sort the cards, arranging them into piles of similar topics.

Sticky Notes or Movable Tape

Like index cards, sticky notes and tape allow you to rearrange your ideas easily. Simply write down an idea on each note or strip of tape and then arrange them on a large piece of paper.

Free Writing

If you can't come up with any ideas using these methods, try simply writing down whatever comes to mind. Later, you can review the text and use an outline to organize the ideas.

GUIDELINES FOR OUTLINING

An outline provides structure and organization. It illustrates the relationship of ideas. It shows you visibly whether you have enough information. In addition, it speeds up the review process when someone in the organization must approve the document.

Outlines can take several different forms. They can vary from the very informal checklist to the formal traditional outline.

The Checklist

Use this system to generate and arrange your ideas. The checklist should include a list of words and phrases that cover key points, with space to insert examples, facts, and other supporting material as you go along.

The Semiformal Outline

This is a compromise between the standard outline and the checklist. In a semiformal outline, you show major ideas and the levels of ideas subordinate to them. You may choose to use capitalization, dashes, numbers, indentations, or other means to show the relationships between ideas.

The Traditional Outline

The traditional outline has a formal framework of Roman and Arabic numerals and uppercase and lowercase letters, arranged with indentations and headings of equal importance. It can be written by hand or on the computer, using the outline view in Microsoft Word. The advantage of using a computer in the outlining stage is that it allows you to see your ideas as they occur and to reorganize them easily.

The Electronic Outline

The larger the amount of information you're including in your document, the harder it is to organize. Outlining software can be a useful tool. You can find outlining modules in word processing programs like Microsoft Word and in presentation packages like Microsoft PowerPoint. Outlining software packages, including Maxthink for PCs and OmniOutliner for the Apple Mac, are also available.

Turning Generated Ideas into an Outline

What steps are involved in going from brainstorming techniques like mind mapping, sticky notes, or free writing to writing an outline?

1. Record random ideas quickly into a nonlinear (messy) outline.
2. Show relationships. Locate the three or four main points. Then draw lines to connect these main points to their supporting points.
3. Arrange the points in an order that makes sense.
4. Draft a final outline. Make sure that you include the following features:
    - *Depth.* Be sure the entire outline has enough support to develop the draft.
    - *Balance*. Include enough detail for all of your main points.
    - *Parallel form*. Give points in the same grouping the same grammatical form.

Whatever system you use to generate and organize your ideas, don't hesitate to revise and reorganize the outline as writing proceeds. An outline is only a guide; you should not feel constricted by it.

NOTES

1. Plain Language Action and Information Network, "Using Writer-Friendly Documents." Online at www.plainlanguage.gov (accessed January 2013).
2. Tony Buzan, *The Mind Map Book* (New York: Penguin, 1991).

Chapter 3

DRAFTING: WRITING IT DOWN

Now that you know what you're going to write, the ideas to include, and the order in which to include them, it's time to put your plan into action.

In writing your first draft, you'll be focusing on paragraphs and sentences. You'll need to organize the paragraphs and structure the sentences in your writing in a way that clearly conveys your message and ideas.

TURNING OFF YOUR INNER CRITIC

Plunge into your first draft with the goal of putting your thoughts in writing. Leave concerns about tone, word choice, spelling, and grammar to the editing stage. Right now, the most important thing is to get into the flow of writing. If you can't think of a particular word to use, leave a blank space. You can always fill it in later.

PLANNING PARAGRAPHS

A well-written paragraph helps the reader by breaking down complex ideas into manageable parts, focusing attention on one idea at a time and relating each part to the main idea of the document.

A well-developed paragraph does not need to be long. Paragraphs should be long enough to make their point adequately—and no longer. If your paragraph is more than 10 to 12 lines, consider breaking it into two or more paragraphs, even if it develops a single idea. Many writers recommend that paragraphs be no longer than five or six lines.

Effective paragraphs have several characteristics:

- *Unity.* Each element of the paragraph contributes to the main idea; nothing irrelevant is included.

- *Coherence.* The parts of the paragraph relate clearly to each other, with each element leading logically to the next.
- *Development.* The main idea is well supported with details—facts, examples, and reasons.

Unity

A unified paragraph is limited to one idea. This makes your document clearer and gives it a cleaner look.

The Need for a Topic Sentence

The topic sentence summarizes and introduces what the paragraph is about. The rest of the paragraph develops the major theme presented in the topic sentence.

Your reader is usually best served if you put the topic sentence first in the paragraph. This practice shortens reading time. The reader does not have to look through the paragraph to find its main point. Also, the reader can skim the topic sentences of all the paragraphs to get the gist of the entire document.

> **Manager Alert**
>
> Your reader is usually best served if you put the topic sentence first in the paragraph.

How to Develop the Topic Sentence

If you have already written a paragraph and need to create a topic sentence for it, identify the main idea and write a sentence describing it. Answering the questions who, what, when, where, why, and how can also help in developing the topic sentence.

The following are examples of effective topic sentences:

- *Ginnie Maes can provide worry-free investment income.*
- *Capital spending increased dramatically in November.*
- *The new software program provides three major benefits.*

Coherence

A paragraph is coherent if the reader can see how it holds together without having to puzzle out the writer's reasons for adding each new sentence. Within a paragraph, as within an entire written message, a logical movement or progression should be apparent.

Using Transitional Devices for Continuity

Conjunctions (such as *and*, *but*, and *or*) and transition words (such as *therefore* and *however*) help readers follow the flow of ideas in a paragraph or between paragraphs. The following are some relationships and the transition words that can express them:

- Contrast—however, although, but, conversely, nevertheless, yet, still, on the other hand, even so, even though, in contrast, in spite of, on the contrary, regardless, otherwise
- Comparison—similarly, likewise, in the same way
- Cause and effect—as a result, therefore, consequently, thus, so, because
- Example—for instance, for example, specifically, as an illustration
- Addition—moreover, besides, in addition, also, too, furthermore
- Time—now, later, after, before, meanwhile, following, then
- Sequence—first, second, third, next, last, finally
- Place—further on, above, below, nearly, on the left, behind, around
- Repetition or summation—all in all, in conclusion, in summary, in other words.

Using Reference Words and Repetition for Linkage

Use reference words such as *this*, *that*, *these*, *those*, and other demonstrative pronouns to tie in new ideas with points made earlier. Also, link your ideas by repeating the topic or key words. For example, if you are writing a report on the benefits of a software program, you might repeat the word "benefit" in each paragraph as a cue to the reader that you are continuing the main idea.

Development

A paragraph can be unified and coherent but still be inadequate. This is because some writers fail to substantiate ideas with supporting facts and explanations. Their readers become interested in the subject, only to be disappointed when no further information is provided. Other writers get so carried away with a subject that they give too much information and bore their readers.

You need to find a way to develop your ideas adequately but not excessively.

A well-developed paragraph provides the specific information readers need and expect to understand and to stay interested in what you're saying. You might want to develop and arrange the information according to a specific pattern.

WRITING SENTENCES

When constructing sentences, be careful to avoid two common problems: sentence fragments and run-on sentences. Review the grammar rules and, if in doubt, have someone review your writing to identify any problems with sentence structure.

You also want to make your sentences clear, readable, and interesting. To do that, vary the structure as well as the length of your sentences. Avoid overloaded or choppy sentences.

Overloaded Sentences

The following sentence is not, strictly speaking, grammatically incorrect. But it does impede the reader's understanding by piling up too many ideas, one after the other.

> *The statements were made by Richard N. Wilson, Project Director for the Southern Regional Center, a federally funded, department-sponsored project that does research for participating agencies in Region IV, a region that includes Kentucky, Tennessee, North Carolina, South Carolina, Georgia, Alabama, Mississippi, and Florida.*

The writer of this sentence has ignored natural stopping places and has tied together ideas that should be expressed in separate sentences. Shorter sentences break the information into smaller, easier-to-process units. Therefore, they are better for conveying complex information. Vary your sentences to avoid choppiness, but don't revert to overloaded sentences like this.

Choppy Sentences

Choppiness results from too many short sentences, lack of sentence transition, and unvaried sentence patterns. Such writing can be monotonous and even irritating, because we all need variety.

> *Read this paragraph out loud. It sounds choppy. The style seems immature. It sounds as if it was written by an 8-year-old. The writing is boring. It is monotonous.*[1]

Contrast the paragraph above with the following paragraph:

> *If you read this paragraph out loud, you'll realize that it sounds choppy. The style seems immature, as though it were written by an 8-year-old. It's boring and monotonous.*[2]

To overcome choppiness, try the following:

- Vary sentence beginnings. The first paragraph above sounds choppy because most of the sentences begin with the subject. To alleviate this repetitious pattern, try one of the following suggestions:
    - Open with a descriptive word (a modifier). *"Strangely, the government did not give liberal leave during last week's snowstorm."*

- Open with a descriptive phrase (a modifier). *"Despite my better judgment, I let Harold take over the project."*
- Open with a subordinate clause (a dependent word group with a subject and verb). *"When Congress announced its budget reform package, members of both political parties offered their support."*
- Open with an infinitive ("to" plus a verb). *"To protect our resources, we must make recycling a way of life."*

- Vary the placement of transitions (words and phrases that link ideas).
  - Place the transition at the beginning: *"In addition, providing child care in the workplace is a good idea, because half of all mothers work."*
  - Place it in the middle: *"Jan's opinion, on the other hand, is that child-care programs will cost too much money."*
  - Place it at the end: *"Many employers now offer day care as a benefit, however."*
- Combine short sentences that relate in content.
  - Before: *"The Recreation Division will close its Central City offices next fall. The closing will occur because of downsizing."*
  - After: *"Next fall, because of downsizing, the Recreation Division will close its Central City offices."*
- Vary the length of your sentences.
  - *"This office needs a director who knows how to deal effectively with upper management and how to trim waste from the budget. This office needs Lee Johnson."*
  - Use your ear. Read your paragraphs aloud. When you hear that the sentences are not flowing well, place a check mark. Then go back and use the techniques just described to ease the flow.[3]

TIPS FOR WRITING DRAFTS

To make the draft stage easier and more productive, consider the following steps:

- Once you have a complete outline in hand, write your first draft quickly.
- Schedule blocks of uninterrupted time for drafting.
- Begin with the easiest section.
- After you complete the first draft, walk away from it.
- After you get some distance, take a few minutes to review your draft with fresh eyes.
- Assess the following before going into the editing stage:
  - Did I explain my purpose clearly?

- Did I consider the role, knowledge level, attitude, and other characteristics of the reader?
- Does the overall organization of the draft make sense?
- Did I provide closure? (For example, did you tell readers exactly what you want them to do?)

After taking a cursory look at your first draft, you're ready to go on to the editing stage.

NOTES

1. Barbara Fine Clouse, *Working It Out: A Troubleshooting Guide for Writers*, 2nd ed. (New York: McGraw-Hill, 1997), 90.
2. Ibid.
3. Ibid., 91–93.

Chapter 4

EDITING: USING THE RIGHT VOICE AND TONE

Voice and tone can either strengthen or weaken the impact of writing. Using the active voice, selecting strong verbs, and deciding on the right intonation can make a world of difference in your day-to-day writing as a government manager.

PREFER THE ACTIVE VOICE

We often lessen the impact of our writing by using the passive voice.

In an active sentence, the person or agency performing an action is the subject of the sentence. In a passive sentence, the person or item acted upon is the subject of the sentence.

Changing passive voice to active voice in your writing can add energy and cut wordiness. Consider the following two versions of the same basic message, which describes a supervisor's actions:

> *All issues and questions were discussed and explained very clearly by my supervisor. Following the completion of each task, I received a full feedback that gave me an opportunity to reflect upon and improve my performance. I was given support in addressing my personal objectives such as improvement of interviewing skills and building technical and client knowledge.*
>
> ...
>
> *My supervisor clearly explained all the issues and fully answered my questions. His comments after every task helped me to reflect upon and improve my performance. He constantly encouraged me to address my objectives, such as improving my interviewing skills and building my technical knowledge.*

The first version, in passive voice, is wordier, weaker, and less direct. The second version, in active voice, is briefer, clearer, and more conversational or natural.

How to Recognize Passive and Active Sentences

The active voice emphasizes who is doing something:

> *"My supervisor clearly explained all the issues and fully answered my questions."*

The actor (my supervisor) comes first in the sentence. The subject of the sentence does the action.

The passive voice emphasizes who or what is being acted upon:

> *"All issues and questions were discussed and explained very clearly by my supervisor."*

Or, the doer may not be mentioned in the passive sentence:

> *"All issues and questions were discussed and explained very clearly."*

Passive sentences have two basic features (although they do not occur in every passive sentence):

1. Some form of "to be" as a helping verb
2. A *past participle* (usually with "ed" on the end).

Passive voice:

- "The checks *have been mailed*."
- "Regulations *have been proposed* by the Department of Veterans Affairs."
- "You *were asked* by me."
- "Copies *are prepared* downstairs."

Active voice:

- "We **mailed** the checks."
- "We **have proposed** regulations."
- "I **asked** you."
- "Mark and Heather **prepare** copies downstairs."

Often the word "by" appears after the verb in a passive sentence to show who performs the action of the verb.

- Passive voice: *"The speech was given by the director."*
- Active voice: *"The director gave the speech."*

How to Activate Passive Sentences

To communicate effectively, write most of your sentences in the active voice. To change passive sentences to active, follow these four steps:

1. Find or supply the actors.

"An excellent job was done by Stacy." *Stacy* is the actor.

2. Put the actor at the beginning of the sentence.

   "Stacy . . ."

3. Replace the passive verb with an active verb.

   "Stacy did . . ."

4. Make the subject of the passive sentence the direct object.

   "Stacy did an excellent job."

> **MANAGER ALERT**
>
> Sometimes the passive voice is a better choice, such as when you need to point out an error or shortcoming in a diplomatic way. "A mistake was made in the last set of calculations" is more tactful than "You made a mistake in the last set of calculations."

BRING SUBMERGED ACTION TO THE SURFACE

Verbs give action to sentences. Submerged verbs are those combined with auxiliary or other weak verbs and turned into nouns. Submerged verbs often occur in connection with the weak verbs "to be," "to make," and "to do."

Weak: *"The accountants do careful work in getting out the final numbers."*

Stronger: *"The accountants work carefully in getting out the final numbers."*

Weak: *"We will give consideration to your idea."*

Stronger: *"We will consider your idea."*

Weak: *"The function of this office is the collection of accounts."*

Stronger: *"This office collects accounts."*

Other weak verb forms can also submerge the action.

SUBSTITUTE ACTION VERBS FOR FORMS OF "TO BE"

Forms of "to be" ("am," "is," "are," "was," "were") have less energy and interest than action verbs do. Whenever possible, opt for action verbs.

Less energy: *"My boss was always a believer in empowerment."*

More energy: *"My boss always believed in empowerment."*

Trying to avoid forms of the verb "to be" might even force you to become creative and descriptive:

Less energy: "After the office social, people were happier."

More energy: "After the office party, people *smiled, chatted,* and *thanked* the members of the Social Committee."

CHOOSE THE APPROPRIATE TONE

The appropriate tone for most government business writing conveys friendliness, concern, and respect—without being overly familiar or ingratiating, and without hedging.

Government and general business writing is becoming more informal, friendly, and straightforward. Nevertheless, an element of judgment is usually involved in finding the right tone. You need to judge, for example, when a personal expression is just right and when a reflection of your personality, opinions, and feelings would be distracting or embarrassing. You need to judge when you're being businesslike at the cost of being friendly.

Finding the right tone is not always easy, but it helps to think from the standpoint of your reader. Some methods for finding the right tone include:

- Use "you," "your," or "yours" to address your reader personally and add immediacy to your letter or report. One of the worst tone offenses in government writing is to refer to people as if they were inanimate objects. Notice the difference between these two sentences:
    - The leg injury is disabling; therefore, the payee is entitled to benefits.
    - We found that *you* have a disabling leg injury; therefore, *you* are entitled to benefits.

The two changes to the second sentence are the use of "you" and the active voice.

- Use "I" or, if you are writing on behalf of your organization, use "we." Let the reader know that a human is writing, not a machine.
    - *I* look forward to seeing you at the conference.
    - *We'll* let you know when we receive your application.
- Also use "I" to:
    - Write in a less negative or accusatory tone
    - Soften the blow of unpleasant news.
- Say "please," "thanks," and "thank you" where appropriate.
    - *Please* fill out the form so we can send you the reimbursement check.
    - *Thank you* for letting us know your change of address.

- Use *italics*, ALL CAPS, or **bold** type sparingly, if at all, to emphasize points.
- Refrain from using exclamation points.
- When you have to communicate bad news or a disappointing response, try to put yourself in the reader's place. Try to convey friendliness, concern, and warmth. Or try to defuse the situation. Don't argue with the reader—just supply the information needed to clarify points that might be confusing or misleading.
    - Instead of: *"You are not qualified for this benefit."*
    - Try: *"Unfortunately, you do not qualify for this benefit."*
- Use "must" to indicate requirements. Avoid using "shall" or "should" where possible.
    - *"The governor must approve it."*
- If you're saying no and asking for a response, be sure to state the benefits of responding.
    - *"We will process your order as soon as we receive your check."*
- If you're writing to complain, state facts and avoid emotion—which is not easy to do when you're angry. Probably the most effective approach is to be firm and specific while keeping a sense of humor.
- If an apology is called for, make it—without groveling or hedging. Apologize at once, for something specific, in as few words as possible.
    - Instead of: *"Rest assured that we deeply regret the inconvenience our error has possibly caused you."*
    - Try: *"Thanks for informing us of the error. We hope it has not inconvenienced you."*
- Where appropriate, end on a positive note by mentioning corrective action.
    - *"We're sending the balance of your refund today."*
- Sometimes you need to qualify a statement; in those cases, words like "apparently" and "in general" are appropriate. But if you use such words habitually, your writing will have a hedging tone and imply that you aren't quite sure about what you're saying. Here are some qualifying words and phrases to watch out for:
    - apparently
    - in general
    - ordinarily
    - as a rule
    - in many instances
    - seems to indicate
    - as a usual case
    - in most cases
    - seemingly
    - commonly
    - it appears
    - usually
    - generally
    - normally

- Use neutral or positive language that puts the situation in the best light.
    - Instead of: *"Because you failed to set up a team meeting, we must postpone the next phase of the ABC Project."*
    - Try: *"We will proceed with the next phase of the ABC Project after you set up a team meeting."*
- When you can convey good news, make it sound good.
    - Instead of: *"This letter will inform you that you will be sponsored as this staff's representative to the annual meeting."*
    - Try: *"Congratulations! Staff members have chosen you to represent them at the annual meeting."*
- Be sincere. Don't gush. Don't lead the reader to question your credibility.
    - Instead of: *"The response was fantastic."*
    - Try: *"Your idea received overwhelming support. The managers voted to feature it at the next staff meeting."*
- Don't make it seem as if you're talking down to your reader.
    - Instead of: *"You realize, obviously, that those results couldn't possibly be valid. It is well known, of course, that . . ."*
    - Try: *"These results may not be valid."*

Take the time to examine your documents through the eyes of your readers. Using active voice and a professional, friendly tone can determine whether they read—and act on—your message.

Chapter 5

EDITING: WRITING WITH CLARITY AND CONCISENESS

Messages written in plain language are much more likely to be read, understood, and heeded—in much less time. Your reader should not have to muddle through confusing, excess verbiage to discover your meaning. Readers who become frustrated by unclear writing might not read a document at all. Whether you're writing to the general public or to members of your agency's staff, clarity and conciseness will help you get your message across.

IMPROVING CLARITY

To improve the clarity of your document, use short sentences, divide material into lists whenever possible, replace wordy expressions, relax old-fashioned grammar rules, avoid cumbersome phrases, delete redundancies, use shorter words when possible, and use parallelism.

Use Short Sentences

Many documents are never read or understood because of long, confusing sentences. Short sentences break information into small, easy-to-process units. They also add vigor and clarity to your documents, helping hold the reader's interest.

The following is an example of a complex sentence that was divided into four shorter, clearer sentences:

Before	After
For good reasons, the Secretary may grant extensions of time in 30-day increments for filing of the lease and all required bonds, provided that additional extension requests are submitted and approved before the expiration of the original 30 days or the previously granted extension.	We may extend the time you have to file the lease and required bonds. Each extension will be granted for a 30-day period. To get an extension, you must write to us, giving the reason that you need more time. We must receive your extension request in time to approve it before your current deadline or extension expires.

In the following example, the "if" clause was made into a separate sentence:

Before	After
If you take less than your entitled share of production for any month, but you pay royalties on the full volume of your entitled share in accordance with the provisions of this section, you will owe no additional royalty for that lease of prior periods when you later take more than your entitled share to balance your account. This also applies when the other participants pay you money to balance your account.	Suppose that one month you pay royalties on your full share of production but take less than your entitled share. In this case, you may balance your account in one of the following ways without having to pay more royalty: (a) take more than your entitled share in the future, or (b) accept money from other participants.

Note that in this example, the writer began the first sentence with "suppose that" and the second sentence with "in this case" to preserve the relationship between the two sentences.

Divide Material Into Lists

If you have a complex paragraph with several parts, you can help your reader by dividing the parts into a list. A numbered or bulleted list will help your reader locate the information more easily and focus on each idea separately.

Vertical lists do the following:

- Highlight levels of importance
- Help the reader understand the order in which things happen
- Make it easy for the reader to identify all necessary steps in a process
- Add blank space for easy reading
- Are an ideal way to present items, conditions, and exceptions.

Here's an example from the PLAIN website:[1]

Before	After
Each completed well drilling application must contain a detailed statement including the following information: the depth of the well, the casing and cementing program, the circulation media (mud, air, foam, etc.), the expected depth and thickness of freshwater zones, and well site layout and design.	With your application for a drilling permit, provide the following information: • Depth of the well • Casing and cementing program • Circulation media (mud, air, foam, etc.) • Expected depth and thickness of freshwater zones • Well site layout and design

Be careful not to overuse vertical lists. Use them to highlight important information, not to overemphasize trivial matters. If you use bullets, use round or square ones. Large, creative bullets with strange shapes tend to distract the reader.

Replace Wordy Expressions

Many expressions that were once considered standard business English or legal expressions today sound stiff, stale, or pompous.

The following list shows how to update some worn-out expressions. Many of these alternatives will improve your style and prevent confusion.

Instead of	Try
aforementioned	omit; or say "the [ ] I mentioned"
allow me to point out; permit me to point out	please note
are in receipt of	received
as per your request	regarding your request
at an early date	soon; by [exact date]
at this time; at this point in time; at the present time	now
at this writing; as of this writing	omit; or say "now"
avail yourself of the opportunity	omit; or say "find time to" or "get the chance"
at your earliest convenience	omit; or say "as soon as you can" or "by [specific date]"

Instead of	Try
be of service to you	serve you; help you
contents noted	omit
desirous of	wish to
during such time as	when, while
enclosed please find/attached please find	see the copy I've enclosed; the enclosed copy shows
feel	unless you're expressing an emotion, use "think" or "believe"
for your information	omit
I have before me your letter	omit
I remain	omit
in a hasty manner	hastily; quickly
in compliance with your request	as you requested
a check in the amount of	a check for [amount]; a [amount] check
in the event that	if
in the near future	specify when
kindly	please
legal terms: hereto, herewith, hereby, hereinafter, said, etc.	within, with this, etc.
please be advised that	omit; or say "note that"
pursuant to your request; in reference to your request	refer to previous correspondence more directly (e.g., "we received your March 8 request")
recent date	specify date
referenced letter	the letter; the letter of [specified date]
regret to inform you	sorry to tell you
relative to	about
same (e.g., "we have cashed same")	specify what "same" is (e.g., the check)

Instead of	Try
subject; employee	he; she
take the liberty of (telling you)	omit; or say "we'd like to tell you"
take this opportunity to	omit; get to the subject
thanking you in advance	presumptuous; say "I will appreciate if you will [action]"
the writer(s)	I/we
the undersigned	I/we
this letter will acknowledge	omit; get to the point
trusting you will; trusting this is	omit; introduces doubt
under separate cover	in another envelope; in an express mail letter, etc.
we wish to state	we believe; we want to assure you

Relax Old-Fashioned Grammar Rules

Some of what we've been taught to think of as rules of grammar are really matters of usage; that is, of what is considered acceptable in using our language. Here are some rules that have now been relaxed or done away with:

- Don't use contractions in business writing. Today, using words like "it's," "don't," we're," and "here's" is acceptable and often even advisable. These words help us cut through formality and make our writing friendly in tone.
- Never start a sentence with "and" or "but." Today, accepted English usage recognizes that starting a sentence with one of these words might be highly effective—or weak. Writers are allowed to follow their instincts.
- Never end a sentence with a preposition. Current opinion says that this rule is one you don't have to adhere to.

Avoid Cumbersome Phrases

Many writers think that using more words will elevate their style or be more proper for business correspondence. They use phrases when a word will do; they use expressions that are roundabout rather than to the point. The result is writing that is officious, cumbersome, and often confusing—a chore to read. Consider this one:

> *"Please be advised that, in the event of fire, employees should avail themselves of the opportunity to exit via . . . ."*

Some cumbersome expressions and suggested remedies follow.

Instead of	Try
adversely impact on	hurt
a large percentage of	many
a total of $250	$250
be in possession of	have
be of the opinion that	believe, think
despite the fact that	though
due to the fact that	due to, since, because
during which time	while
endeavor to ascertain	try to find out
exhibits a tendency to	tends to
for a period of a month	for a month
for the purpose of	to, for
give consideration to	consider
have occasion to be	have reason to be
has a requirement for	requires
in accordance with	by, following, under
in the majority of instances	often, usually
in the month of April	in April
in a number of cases	sometimes
in reference to	about
in the near future	soon
in the neighborhood of	about
in the field of economics	in economics
in view of the fact that	in view of, since
is authorized to	may
make an appearance	appear

Instead of	Try
not in a position	unable
on or before	by
range all the way from	range from
subsequent to	after
there are many people who think that	many people think
until such time	when
we deem it advisable	we suggest
with a view to	to
with regard to	about
without further delay	now

Delete Redundancies

Redundant writing repeats itself; it says, unintentionally, the same thing twice. Redundancies often creep in when we feel compelled to pad our writing with filler phrases, such as those shown in parentheses below:

"He was named (to the position of) director last week."

"We hope to see you (at an) early (time)."

"The man is unusual (in nature) but honest (in character)."

Sometimes redundancies emerge when we try too hard to make things absolutely clear. It's all too easy to say

"After our boss reviewed the (important) essentials, she gave us an (unexpected) surprise."

"We will hear the (final) outcome tonight."

The following are some common redundant expressions. The words in parentheses are unnecessary.

Noun Forms	Verb Forms	Adjective and Other Forms
(total) annihilation	appoint (to the position of)	adequate (enough)
(major) breakthrough	ascend (up)	big (in size)
capitol (building)	attach (together)	(entirely) complete

Noun Forms	Verb Forms	Adjective and Other Forms
(fellow) colleague	climb (up)	contemporary (in time)
(final) completion	coalesce (together)	each (and every)
consensus (of opinion)	combine (together)	(all) finished
(mutual) cooperation	commute (back and forth)	first (and foremost)
courthouse (building)	congregate (together)	(exactly) identical
(general) custom	continue (on, still)	large (in stature)
(doctorate) degree	continue (to remain)	never (at any time)
(complete) destruction	cooperate (jointly)	(more) preferable
(baffling) dilemma	cover (over)	same (identical)
(sudden) eruption	depreciated (in value)	sufficient (enough)
(necessary) essential	descend (down)	(completely) unanimous
(passing) fad	eliminate (entirely)	unless (and until)
(basic) fundamentals	follow (after)	whether (or not)
(opening) gambit	gather (together)	
(free) gift	join (together)	
(past) history	may (possibly)	
(present) incumbent	merge (together)	
(new) innovation	name (as, to the position of)	
lawyer (by occupation)	penetrate (into)	
twelve o'clock (midnight)	(continue to) persist	
(personal) opinion	(pre) plan	
complete (monopoly)	prejudge (in advance)	
(final) outcome	recall (back)	
(fellow) partner	recur (again)	
(advance) planning	revert (back)	
(troublesome) predicament	skirt (around)	

Noun Forms	Verb Forms	Adjective and Other Forms
(leading) protagonist	spell out (in detail)	
(original) prototype		
(temporary) reprieve		
(local) resident		
(end) result		

Use Shorter Words

Overblown words distract readers. Readers might end up paying more attention to how you're saying it than to what you're saying. And they might lose interest, especially if they have to look up words they don't know. Some inflated words and their deflated equivalents follow.

Instead of	Try
accompanied	went with
accomplished	done
activate	begin
advantageous	helpful
aggregate	total
ameliorate	improve
approximately	about
ascertain	find
assist	help
categorize	sort
commence	start
communicate	write, tell
construct	make
demonstrate	show
discontinue	stop
disseminate	give, issue, send

Instead of	Try
edifice	building
encounter	meet
endeavor	try
examination	test
expedite	hasten, hurry up
facilitate	ease, simplify
indicate	show
initial	first
initiate	begin
modification	change
promulgate	publish
procure	get, buy
reside	live
terminate	end, stop
utilize	use

Use Parallelism

Making the parts parallel means using the same grammatical construction and beginning with the same part of speech. Simply put, ideas that look roughly alike in your mind should look roughly alike on the page. In grammar, this is called parallel construction.

Dr. Martin Luther King, Jr., in his "I Have a Dream" speech, used both repetition and parallel construction effectively:

> *Now is the time to make real the promises of democracy. Now is the time to rise from the dark and desolate valley of segregation to the sunlit path of racial justice. Now is the time to open the doors of opportunity to all of God's children. Now is the time to lift our nation from the quicksands of racial injustice to the solid rock of brotherhood.*[2]

The following familiar phrases also illustrate the use of parallel construction:

> *"One if by land, two if by sea."*
>
> *"Where there's a will, there's a way."*

"Saw sub, sank same."

"Ask not what your country can do for you; ask what you can do for your country."

Even if you're uncertain of the grammar principles involved, you can usually detect nonparallel items by using your ear. Nonparallel passages sound awkward. Read the following statements:

Nonparallel	Parallel
The new copier is efficient, easy to operate, and it is relatively inexpensive.	The new copier is efficient, easy to operate, and relatively inexpensive.
The steel companies lost money because of high costs, foreign competition had increased, and they had inefficient processes.	The steel companies lost money because of high costs, increased foreign competition, and inefficient processes.
The trip will involve traveling by airplane, bus, and by car.	The trip will involve traveling by airplane, bus, and car.

There are specific ways to diagnose problems with parallelism, or to match the parts. Some common problems are:

- Using the wrong part of speech
  - Unmatched: *"He acted quickly and with care."*
  - Matched: *"He acted quickly and carefully."*
- Shifting from active to passive voice.
  - Unmatched: *"The company finished the job on time, but many errors were made by its workers."*
  - Matched: *"The company finished the job on time, but its workers made many errors."*
- Shifting person
  - Unmatched: *"When you leave our building, take a left; then I usually go three blocks and take a right."* (third person, first person)
  - Matched: *"When you leave our building, take a left; then go three blocks and take a right."* (second person, second person)

Lists are much easier to read when the items they contain are parallel. In the list on the left, three of the items begin with adverbs (what, when, and where), two begin with gerunds (getting, eating), and one begins with a noun (passport). In the list on the right, each item begins with a noun.

Nonparallel	Parallel
• passport	• passport
• what to wear and pack	• clothing
• where to stay	• hotels
• getting around the city	• transportation
• when and where workshops meet	• workshops
• eating out	• restaurants

Parallel construction makes the passage shorter and clearer. It also demonstrates both logic and attention to detail.

Follow Guidelines for Writing Clearly

Some simple guidelines will also help you make your writing clear:

- *If you use an acronym (abbreviation) your readers might not know, spell it out the first time you use it.* An example is "Department of Labor (DOL) contractors . . . ." Do not abbreviate terms you use only once or a few times. Write them out each time.
- *Use the same term consistently to identify a specific thought or object.* For example, if you use the term "senior citizens" to refer to a group, continue to use this term throughout your document. Do not substitute another term, such as "the elderly"—your reader may wonder if you are referring to the same group.[3]
- *Avoid jargon whenever possible.* Jargon is the specialized vocabulary and idioms shared by those in the same organization or profession. If a scientific, technical, or legal term is the best word to describe what you mean, use it. If you think your reader might be unfamiliar with the term, define it the first time you use it.

BEING PRECISE

Read the following paragraph:

> *Participants in the seminar said the curriculum related to the major responsibilities involved in their employment. They indicated that they had obtained information that would enable them to perform their obligations. One participant noted that the seminar design provided for concentration on certain areas for a given length of time.*

Hard to grasp? The paragraph is a model of imprecision. You can't read it and get a clear picture of what happened at the seminar; all you can do is try to interpret its meaning.

Now read the following paragraph and compare it to the original:

> *Nearly 85 percent of participants in the project management seminar said the curriculum covered the major responsibilities in their positions, including project planning, scheduling, and control. They said they had learned about calculating cost and schedule variances that would enable them to deal with unexpected changes in their projects. One participant noted that the seminar design provided for three hours of concentration in critical path scheduling.*

This version of the paragraph gives much more specific information and is more persuasive. Precise words that give solid evidence help you convince the reader.

Being precise and readable can be a challenge. Depending on your subject matter and audience, you sometimes must make tradeoffs.

When you're writing about requirements, for example, use singular nouns and verbs to prevent confusion about whether a requirement applies to individual readers or to groups.

- Imprecise: "*Individuals and organizations wishing to apply must file applications with the appropriate offices in a timely manner.*"
- Precise: "*You must apply at least 30 days before you need the certification:*
  - *(a) If you are an individual, apply at the state office in the state where you reside.*
  - *(b) If you are an organization, apply at the state office in the state where your headquarters is located.*"

AVOIDING COMMON BARRIERS TO UNDERSTANDING

It's always a good idea to read over what you've written. Put yourself in the reader's place. How do you sound? Clear, forceful, and lively? Sure of yourself? Firm but friendly? Intelligent but not arrogant?

The following are suggestions for diagnosing and remedying some of the common barriers.

Watch Out for "Noun Sandwiches"

Sometimes you must break the rule about being concise. The following group of words would trip up most readers:

> "*underground mine worker safety procedures development*"

The tight knot of thoughts ("noun sandwich") needs to be loosened by adding prepositions and articles to clarify relationships among the words:

> *"development of safety procedures to protect workers in underground mines"*

Place Words Carefully Within Your Sentences

Keep subjects and objects close to their verbs. The following sentence is both long and poorly constructed:

> *"The project leader, after hearing all the results of the annual evaluation and weighing the pros and cons of the evaluation team's recommendations, decided to make five major changes in the program."*

By the time readers get to the verb "decided," they may have forgotten that the subject is "project leader." Try this:

> *"After hearing all the results of the annual evaluation and weighing the pros and cons of the evaluation team's recommendations, the project leader decided to make five major changes in the program."*

Better still, put the ideas into two short sentences.

> *"The project leader heard the results of the annual evaluation and weighed the pros and cons of the evaluation team's recommendations. He then decided to make five major changes in the program."*

Put conditionals like "only" or "always" and other modifiers next to the words they modify.

- Ambiguous: *"You are only required to provide the following."*
- Clear: *"You are required to provide only the following."*

Make Pronoun References Clear

Have you cleared up any questions about which words your pronouns stand for? (In grammatical terms, have you cleared up any faulty references?)

- Ambiguous: *"The agencies have a number of field offices. Most of the work is done in them."*
- Clear: *"The agencies have a number of field offices. Most of the work is done in these offices."*

Correct Dangling Modifiers

Have you made sure there are no dangling modifiers to confuse (or amuse) the reader?

- Dangling: *"Here are some tips for protecting your valuables from our security staff."*

Members of the security staff are not stealing valuables. They are offering tips.

- Clear: *"Here are some tips from our security staff for protecting your valuables."*
- Dangling: *"After waiting 10 minutes, the engineer told us the elevator was not working."*

The engineer did not wait 10 minutes. You did.

- Clear: *"After we had waited 10 minutes, the engineer told us the elevator was not working."*

Use Words Correctly

When you're concentrating on getting your thoughts down, it's easy to write one word when you mean another. It's also easy to use words carelessly, letting them slip by even though you're not sure that they're correct in the context.

Many errors are made because we mistake words that look and sound alike, such as:

- assure/ensure/insure
- flout/flaunt
- effect/affect
- site/sight/cite.

These errors can be embarrassing. Readers may understand and give us credit for what we meant to say. Sometimes, however, the misuse of words can mislead or perplex readers:

> *"The idea literally blew them away." (Really? Or did it figuratively blow them away?)*
>
> *"We will not stand for the prosecution (persecution?) of the handicapped."*

CHECKING READABILITY

A document's readability is the level of difficulty at which it is written, and therefore the level of education required to understand it. Readability is based on

- The average length of sentences
- The average number of syllables in a word.

Readability of Familiar Publications[4]	
The Atlantic Monthly	Grade 12 (difficult)
The Wall Street Journal	Grade 11
The New York Times	Grade 10
Los Angeles Times	Grade 10
Business Week	Grade 10
Time magazine	Grade 10
Reader's Digest	Grade 8
Boston Globe	Grade 8
U.S.A. Today	Grade 7
People magazine	Grade 6 (easy)

A document with long sentences and many syllables is considered more difficult to read than one with shorter sentences and fewer syllables. A ninth-grade level is about the right level for most business and government documents. This level uses few long words and keeps sentences to about 15 words in length.

Computer programs, readability graphs, and "Fog" indexes are some of the ways to determine a document's readability. You can calculate the Fog index as follows:[5]

1. Using a sample of at least 100 words, find the average number of words per sentence. Divide the total number of words by the number of sentences. This gives you the average sentence length.
2. Count the number of words of three syllables or more per 100 words. Don't count (a) words that are capitalized; (b) combinations of short, easy words like bookkeeper; and (c) verbs that are made three syllables by adding "ed" or "es"—like "created" or "trespasses."
3. Add the two figures above and multiply by 0.4. This will give you the Fog index. It corresponds roughly with the number of years of schooling a person requires to read a passage with ease and understanding.

MANAGER ALERT

To help your staff improve their writing, teach them how to use the Fog index. This index points out wordiness and the need for simpler language in a direct, impersonal way.

NOTES

1. Plain Language Action and Information Network, "Use Lists." Online at www.plainlanguage.gov (accessed January 2013).
2. Martin Luther King, Jr., "The I Have a Dream Speech." Online at www.usconstitution.net/dream.html (accessed January 2013).
3. Plain Language Action and Information Network, "Use the Same Term Consistently for a Specific Thought or Object." Online at www.plainlanguage.gov (accessed January 2013).
4. Deborah Dumaine, *Write to the Top: Writing for Corporate Success* (New York: Random House, 1989).
5. Robert Gunning, *The Technique of Clear Writing* (New York: McGraw-Hill, 1968).

Chapter 6

EDITING: THE FINAL PHASE

People are often tempted to ignore the final editing phase, but doing so is risky. A thoughtful editorial review is the last line of defense for every document.

It's important to review your work to make sure that your writing achieves its purpose; your ideas are stated clearly and correctly; and your writing is free of spelling, grammatical, and other mechanical errors. Remember, even professional writers rely on editors to cast a critical eye on their work.

TWO TYPES OF EDITING

When we discuss editing, we are really referring to two different types of critical review: substantive editing and line (or copy) editing. In substantive editing, you review the overall development of the writing, looking at how well the ideas are organized and developed and how well they are presented. In line editing, you check subject-verb agreement, verb tense, active and passive voice, understandability, precision, and readability, as well as the mechanics of writing, such as spelling and punctuation.

Substantive Editing

During this step, look at the overall picture. Consider what you've said, and put yourself in the reader's place. Read only what you've put on the page; don't read in what you know but have left unsaid. If possible, have someone who is totally unfamiliar with the subject read what you've written.

The following checklist can help you make sure your writing is doing what you want it to do:

- *Statement of purpose*. Make sure you have stated your purpose and that your ideas and the organization of them help you achieve that purpose.

- *Completeness.* Check your document against your outline to make sure you have covered all points.
- *Unity of thought.* If you have digressed from your outline, decide whether the departure is justified.
- *Redundancy.* Keep a sharp eye out for places where you have repeated yourself.
- *Audience.* Ask yourself if what you have written is understandable and useful to the people who will read it. You want to say enough to inform them without saying too much.
- *The "bottom line on top."* Check that you have put the main idea of your document first. Then check each section to make sure the main idea comes first.
- *Clarity.* Your ideas should be presented clearly and logically; no ideas should be hidden or thrown in at the end without being fully developed.
- *White space.* White space between paragraphs makes each paragraph stand out visually. Indents or bullets help show how ideas are subordinate to each other. In this checklist, for example, bullets show that each item is part of the main checklist.
- *Headings and subheadings.* These should help the reader understand your organization.
- *Conclusions.* Make sure they are understandable and that you said enough to support them—but not too much.
- *Transitional words.* These help the reader see the connections between your ideas.

Line Editing

Once you've looked at the overall picture, it's time to check the details, such as the development of paragraphs and sentences. Now is the time to think about word choice, tone, style, readability, understandability, and precision. As you read over something, think about how it sounds to you.

Line editing also means checking for proper and consistent spelling, punctuation, capitalization, abbreviation, word division, and the like—matters that are sometimes referred to as the mechanics of writing. The purpose of line editing is to eliminate any errors or inconsistencies, as well as any awkward features that might distract the reader from what is being said.

The following checklist can help you with line editing:

- *Paragraphs.* Make sure each paragraph covers one main idea and has a topic sentence that introduces that main idea.

- *Sentences*. Each sentence should cover one idea. If a sentence covers more than one idea, decide if it should it be broken into two sentences. Check to see that sentences are varied in structure and in length.
- *Verbs*. Use the active voice, in which the subject of the sentence performs the action, whenever possible.
- *Submerged verbs*. Look for any verbs that have been submerged under helping verbs and turned into nouns (such as "He made an assessment" instead of "He assessed").
- *Choice of words*. Read your document aloud to see that it is in plain English. Delete or change any of the following:
  - Bureaucratese (e.g., "At this point in time, we estimate that implementing this program will affect. . ." instead of "We now believe this program will affect . . . .")
  - Clichés (e.g., "six of one and half a dozen of another")
  - Gobbledygook (e.g., "electronically adjusted, colorcoded vehicular-flow control mechanism" instead of "traffic light")
  - Coined words (e.g., "ultra-self-orientationability" instead of "ability to orient itself")
- *Tone*. Make sure your words convey the right amount of friendliness and directness. You don't want to sound overly familiar, arrogant, or unsure.
- *Gender-neutral language*. Avoid using "he" when referring to either male or female. Opt for "flight attendant" rather than "stewardess" and "police officer" rather than "policeman."
- *Clarity*. Choose simple, direct phrases and familiar words. Look for any stiff, pompous-sounding expressions. Be careful not to overuse acronyms.
- *Precision*. Make sure you clearly state what you mean. Instead of vague terms ("large book"), use specific words ("559-page novel").
- *Punctuation*. Ensure the correct use of:
  - Commas
  - Semicolons
  - Colons
  - Periods.

THE EDITING PROCESS

When you're ready to move into editing, try to work during the period of the day when you're most alert. For some of us, this is first thing in the morning; for others, it's the afternoon or late at night. Find a quiet place and force yourself to concentrate. Tackle the job systematically. Don't try to see too many things at once.

Professional editors have different methods for organizing their work. Some begin with a very slow read, then go back and read quickly the second time through.[1]

The following is one way to approach the job:

1. Inventory the materials to make sure you have everything.
   a. If there is more than one page:
      - Does each page have a number?
      - Are the pages in order?
   b. If there is more than one part:
      - Are all the parts (attachments, enclosures, appendices, table of contents, bibliography, exhibits, etc.) included and in order?
      - Is each part labeled correctly and clearly?
      - Are titles and headings typed consistently?
      - Are all footnotes or endnotes included?
2. To begin, focus on groups of words in sentences and paragraphs.
   a. The first time through, read only for meaning.
      - Does what is there, on the page, make sense?
      - Has anything been left out?
   b. Next time, check the mechanics.
      - Are the sentences grammatically correct?
      - Is the punctuation correct?
      - Are all references and citations accurate?
3. Now try to focus on individual words.
   a. Are there any typos?
   b. Are the words spelled correctly?
   c. Are the words capitalized correctly and consistently?
   d. Are the words abbreviated correctly and consistently?
   e. Are the words divided correctly and consistently?
   f. Are figures and symbols used correctly and consistently?
4. Now look at the document as a whole.
   a. Are the parts arranged appropriately and evenly on the page?
      - Are the margins adequate?
      - Does the white space reflect the thought structure?
      - Are the indentations consistent?
      - Is the spacing consistent?

> **Manager Alert**
>
> Plan carefully for the editing process. Make sure your staff understands the importance of this task, and ask that you not be interrupted. You might even ask someone to be in charge and field questions while you (ideally) step away from your desk to a quiet spot.

MAKING CHANGES ONLINE

When you're editing online, first make a working copy of each file you plan to edit and save the original files. You need to have a backup copy; you also might need to consult the unedited original files while you're working on the project. Make sure the working files are labeled differently from the original ones so there will be no confusion.

One useful way to edit online is to track your changes using a program that allows changes to show up in red. Typically, insertions are shown underlined and deletions are shown with strikethrough marks. You can choose whether to have these red lines show in a document. If other people edit your work, the highlighted changes can make their job easier—but they can also be confusing and distracting. The tracking feature is a useful tool in the editing process; the writer or reviewer can choose to accept or reject any or all changes.

HOW CAN A STYLE MANUAL HELP?

A style manual provides guidelines for correctness and consistency regarding the mechanics of language. The federal government generally uses the *U.S. Government Printing Office Style Manual*.[2] You're likely to have questions that are not answered in a style manual. Sometimes a good dictionary will help. Other times, you'll have to rely on your preference and judgment. The key is to follow a style consistently.

EDITING SOMEONE ELSE'S WRITING

Editing someone else's writing requires objectivity, maturity, and tact. A writer has put time and effort into creating a document and may feel that his or her ego is on the line when handing it over for editing. As an editor, try to be balanced, specific, constructive, and tactful.

First, make sure you know the author's purpose for writing the document and the audience for whom the document is intended. Determine what level of editing is needed: light, medium, or heavy. This will depend on the quality of the author's writing, the audience, the production schedule, and the size and importance of the document.

Next, check the materials to make sure they're complete. Read the draft once in its entirety before you make any marks on it. Then ask yourself the questions for substantive editing. When you read the draft through again, consider the points related to line editing.

Guidelines for editing someone else's work include:

- Make no change unless you can give a good reason for it.
- Focus on the document and its impact on the intended reader, not on your preferences.
- Use good judgment in responding to what has been written. If a piece of writing is good, return it with a note saying "Nice work" or "Great job."
- If the document needs substantial editing, take the time to talk to the writer. Suggest some changes you think are necessary and explain why. Provide tactful instruction, not scolding, as needed.
- Remember that your job as an editor is to look at a document objectively—something that is impossible for a writer to do.

Whether you are editing your own or someone else's writing, your work is not truly done until you have seen the manuscript through to the end. You need to make sure that the finished product reflects the care that went into planning, writing, and revising.

Double-check the final product for any details that might have slipped by. At this point, it's a good idea to review the manuscript in hard copy to help you spot difficulties.

NOTES

1. For a thorough explanation of the editorial process, see Amy Einsohn's *The Copyeditor's Handbook*, 3rd ed. (Los Angeles: University of California Press, 2011).
2. *The United States Government Printing Office Style Manual*, 30th ed. (Washington, DC: U.S. Government Printing Office, 2000). Online at www.gpo.gov/fdsys/pkg/GPO-STYLEMANUAL-2008/pdf/GPO-STYLEMANUAL-2008.pdf (accessed January 2013).

Chapter 7

EMAILING THE RIGHT MESSAGE

When decisions, directives, orders, and other official news must reach many people at several levels within the organization, email is an efficient vehicle. Even when a message must reach only one person or a small group, sending an email is often wise. An email is a reliable means of:

- Giving specific instructions
- Conveying detailed facts or figures
- Writing a message any time of the day or night
- Replying directly to another person's written or oral request
- Establishing a record to show that certain things have been said or done, or that certain views are held
- Attaching additional information that readers can open if and when they choose.

Sometimes just trying to decipher what someone is trying to say takes the most time. For this reason, careful planning and review of all electronic communication is a must. You need to pay attention to grammar and spelling even though email is informal. Use complete sentences and appropriate capitalization. Taking care with your email messages shows thoughtfulness and consideration—and gets faster results.

The tone of a message is also important. Many relationships have been damaged by emails sent in the heat of anger. Even in unemotional exchanges, readers often misinterpret tone.

Finally, as an email writer you need to be aware of the legal implications of your messages. There is no such thing as a private email. As recent lawsuits have shown, long-forgotten emails can show up in court.

PLANNING EMAIL

Even when the email you plan to write is short and informal, you should resist the temptation to skip over the planning and outlining stage. Take the time to determine your purpose. Think about what effect you hope to have on the reader and what you want the reader to do after reading your message.

Review any helpful materials (earlier emails, other correspondence, policy statements, regulations, or other documents), jot down key facts, and note ideas that come to you. Consider the reader's role, knowledge of the subject matter, and likely reaction to the topic. Also take into account the reader's relationship to you. This will help you craft your message effectively and convey the appropriate tone.

ELEMENTS OF EMAIL

The most important parts of the email are the subject statement and the opening statement. The subject statement tells readers what the email is about and determines whether they will open it immediately. The opening statement conveys the purpose of the email.

Subject Statement

The subject statement is an opportunity to alert the reader immediately to the essence of the email. Many people do not open their emails. They just skim the subject lines to determine which emails are worth their time. Help your readers by creating a subject line that briefly describes the message and helps them understand whether it is a top priority or can wait. The subject line should use only the words necessary to convey the subject clearly, in language the reader will understand. It should include names, titles, dates, and other details where helpful.

Opening Statement

The first paragraph of the email—preferably the first sentence—should state your position or convey your information. Don't make the reader dig to find out what your point is; get right to it:

> *"Please review the attached policy and send me your comments by November 17."*
>
> *"Would you please bring the pie chart to the next team meeting?"*
>
> *"Attached is the information you requested on the public's response to the updated form."*

Include all the important information in the opening, including the answers to what, when, where, who, why, and how. Be careful not to include unnecessary information.

EMAIL ETIQUETTE

Although many standard rules and niceties apply to emails, a few new ones have cropped up to meet the particular needs of this type of communication.

Tone and Style

All the writing principles that apply to letters apply equally to email:

- Adapt your degree of formality to fit the expectations of the intended reader and your purpose.
- Use social conventions: Please, thank you, and a friendly close can make the difference between a cold, brusque tone and a warm, courteous one. Use positive words whenever possible, and keep your messages courteous, direct, and brief.
- If you want the recipient of the email to take action, be sure to state what that action is and when you would like it to occur. Use tact and consideration in framing the request, but be direct and specific about what you want or need.

The Right Recipient and the Right Timing

Communicating to the right person at the right time is just as important when sending an email as it is when sending a letter:

- Send your message to the right person. Make sure your email goes to the person responsible for the activity or function. Do not go over anyone's head. If you don't get results, you should tell the person that you plan to take the matter up with someone in higher authority.
- Send copies to the right people—anyone affected by the subject or interested in it. Also send copies to anyone mentioned in the email and to anyone in a direct line of authority between you and the addressee. Do not waste people's time by sending officewide emails on topics that do not concern most employees.
- When you send an email to a large group, remember that you are sharing private email addresses with the world—addresses that the recipients might prefer not to share. One way to avoid this is to address the email to yourself and put all the recipients on a blind carbon copy (bcc) to preserve their anonymity.
- Prepare your reader for surprising news, especially if it is negative. Call ahead to explain: "You'll be getting an email later today to explain why your budget was cut."

- Send important information to the important people first. Not everyone reads an email when it first arrives. Consider sending critical information a day or so ahead to the key people or to those who would be embarrassed if they did not know about it before others.
- Use care in forwarding emails. If you think there is any chance that the sender would not want the message shared, check before forwarding.

> **Manager Alert**
>
> Hierarchy can be a sticky area, so if you think it's an issue, put the names in the "To" field in the correct order, generally according to rank. You can also go by seniority or familiarity with the issue.

Other Guidelines

Other tips helpful in writing emails include:

- Send only one important point per email. If you cover more than one issue in an email, chances are good that at least one point will be overlooked or forgotten.
- Avoid "screaming." Never write an email using all capital letters.
- Don't designate a message urgent unless it *is* urgent. If something is urgent, consider phoning rather than risking that the recipient won't see it in time.
- Inform email recipients when your message does not require a reply. You can simply add "FYI—no reply needed" to the message.
- Keep attachments to a minimum. The larger the attached document, the longer it takes to download and the more memory space it fills on the recipient's computer.
- Minimize the number of "Thanks!" replies. Such "content-free mail" is not necessary unless (1) the thank-you is really called for, or (2) you need to let the sender know you received the message.
- Be careful when you "Reply All." Make sure that your message is appropriate for every one of the recipients. When you receive a blind carbon copy (bcc), remember that the sender chose not to reveal that you were a recipient. If you use the "Reply All" option, you will disclose to all that you were a recipient of the original email.
- Know when not to write. Highly sensitive or very personal messages are often better communicated in person or off the record. Don't send a message in the heat of anger and avoid critical, gossipy, or sarcastic messages.

- Use bullets or numbers where appropriate. These help readers pick out your key points. Use numbers when some sequence or priority is required. For example, when giving directions, use numbers to indicate the order in which the steps should be carried out.
- Use emphasis when needed—but use it sparingly. Boldface, italic, underlining, and colored text can draw attention to an important point. Overdoing the emphasis overwhelms the message and implies that you don't trust your reader to find the key points.

SECURITY AND PRIVACY ISSUES

Nothing is private. Even when messages are deleted, they can be accessed on the hard drive by software or online services. Before you click "Send," think about the consequences of someone other than the intended recipient—like your boss—reading the message.

Employers believe they have the right to know if you're using their email system for personal messages, and they sometimes check email. The U.S. government often monitors its messages to protect against email that is being sent for illegal purposes.

SOME LANDMINES TO AVOID

Ever since the use of email began, people have been fired for using it incorrectly. Be especially careful when writing emails that include humor or emails that require action.

Humorous email that can be dangerous falls into two categories: office humor (similar to gallows humor) and offensive jokes. Be careful not to make light of a serious situation. Never send racist, sexist, pornographic, or otherwise disparaging email.

If you receive an email, whether you open it or not, you are presumed to have knowledge of it. Therefore, it is especially important to pay attention to any email that raises problems, especially one that alleges wrongdoing or potentially illegal behavior in your workplace. If you are aware of unethical conduct, you must bring that to the attention of management, and you might need to contact your agency counsel.

Manager Alert

If you receive an email, whether you open it or not, you are presumed to have knowledge of it.

As a general rule, never send an email if you would not put the same words in a letter or memo or if you would not want the email to be viewed as part of a lawsuit or investigation.

Chapter 8

WRITING EFFECTIVE LETTERS

Every good letter you write will help your organization build good relations with the public and with other organizations and agencies. A letter is often the first contact—and might be the only contact—a person has with your organization.

HOW TO FORMAT A BUSINESS LETTER

Although some communications can be made informally with a phone call or an email, formal situations call for a letter. Letter writing provides you and the recipient with a record of facts, ideas, concerns, and suggestions. Organizing and expressing your ideas in a letter takes thought and time but is well worth the effort. A well-written letter makes a good impression.

For a business letter, you should use good-quality, white paper or letterhead. If possible, limit the letter to one single-spaced page. Include in your letter all the common components in the proper order:

Return address. Your address or the name and address of the organization you represent. If you're using letterhead, you don't need to add this information.

Date. The date follows the return address. Some style guides suggest that you should skip a line between the return address and the date; others do not. You can state the date as *January 6, 2013*, or, if your agency requires, as *6 January 2013*.

Inside address. Leave two blank lines after the date. Then type the name, organization, and address of the person to whom you are writing. The inside address should include the recipient's title (e.g., Mrs., Ms., Mr., Dr.).

Salutation. For the salutation, type "Dear," follow with the person's title and name, and end with a colon. If you want to convey a friendly, familiar tone, use a comma instead of a colon.

Subject or Reference Line. Type "Re:" and follow the colon with the reference or main purpose of your letter. Place the subject line two lines below the salutation. It's part of the body of the letter, not the heading.

Body. The actual message is contained in the paragraphs between the salutation and the complimentary close—the body of the letter. These paragraphs should be single-spaced, with a blank line between paragraphs. You can indent the first line of each paragraph (indented style) or leave all lines flush left (block style).

Complimentary closing. Leave two spaces after your last body paragraph, and then use a closing, such as "Sincerely yours," "Cordially," or "Respectfully." Note that only the first word of the complimentary close is capitalized. Follow the closing with a comma.

Signature. Write your signature below the closing. Use both your first and last names unless you've established a personal relationship with the person to whom you're writing.

Name and professional title. Four lines after the closing, type your full name. Put your professional title below your name.

End notations. Under the signature block, abbreviations with important functions are often used.

- Initials. If someone other than the writer types the letter, put the writer's initials, then a slash, and then the typist's initials: "JD/MTS" or "jd/mts."
- Copies. If you send a copy of a letter to someone other than the person addressed, use "cc:" and the person's name. For multiple persons, use "cc:" only once and list the persons vertically in alphabetical order or by rank.
- Enclosures. Use "Enc." if you enclose something with the letter and want to make sure the recipient sees it. For more than one enclosure, use Enc. and the number of enclosures—"Enc. 2," for example.

BASIC STEPS IN WRITING BUSINESS LETTERS

Following a few basic rules will help you write better business letters:

- Rule 1. Determine your purpose.
- Rule 2. Identify your audience.
- Rule 3. Know your subject.
- Rule 4. Follow a logical sequence.
- Rule 5. Immediately identify the subject and state your position.
- Rule 6. Create a paragraph for each step in the process.

- Rule 7. Include only what your reader must know to understand, agree, or act.
- Rule 8. End by pointing the way ahead.

Begin the Letter

Get right to the point! Tell the reader immediately why you are writing:

> *"This letter is to inform you that Section 6 of the St. George's Hundred Project has not been accepted by the James City Service Authority for the following reasons:"*
>
> *"The Master Plan for St. George's Hundred Project was approved by the Planning Commission on February 5, 2013."*

Provide a Point of Reference

If you're answering a message from your reader, it's a good idea to provide a point of reference:

> *"Re: Your letter of April 30, 2012"*
>
> *"Re: Application Form XXX-XX-XX"*

Or, refer to the topic of the reader's previous message in the first sentence of your letter:

> *"I am pleased to inform you that your December 5, 2012, application has been approved by our evaluation branch."*

Organize the Body of the Letter

In the body of your letter, you provide information to support the position you stated in the first paragraph. For example, if you're trying to convince upper management to adopt a revised telework policy (a letter of persuasion), you would give your reasons and present the data that support your reasons in the body of your letter.

End the Letter

Give your business letter an "action ending" whenever possible. The ending of your letter should answer the question, "What next?" You state what you want your readers to do, what you plan to do, and the schedule for that action.

What Readers Should Do

> *"Please let me know by July 10 what you decide to do about filling the position. You can reach me during business hours at the phone number below."*
>
> *"I look forward to seeing you at our meeting on September 18. Please call me if you need directions or have any other questions."*

What You Intend to Do

"I'll get in touch with you next week."

"If you approve this plan, I will call and get bids from the three companies next week."

Occasionally, you might just end the letter by saying something like:

"Thank you for bringing this matter to our attention."

"Thank you for taking the time to consider my ideas."

"We regret any inconvenience that we might have caused you."

Never present new ideas or raise new issues in ending a letter. If you hint about topics that you haven't discussed, you will only bewilder and frustrate your reader.

TYPES OF BUSINESS LETTERS

Common types of business letters include letters of persuasion, legal writing, letters of recommendation, and letters accompanying reports. Each of these letters has a specific objective, a particular form of organization, and a distinct tone.

Letters of Persuasion

On occasion, you might need to write a letter asking the recipients to do something—recycle motor oil, use child safety seats, or send in a form, for example. When you write a letter of persuasion, it's a good idea to follow the model used for sales letters:

- Open with a device to get the reader's attention:
    - Involve the reader in some way
    - Offer a benefit
    - Make a startling statement or present a surprising statistic
    - Ask a rhetorical question.
- Use the body of the letter to:
    - Show how the proposal will benefit the reader
    - Explain exactly what you have in mind
    - Emphasize the main features of the proposal.
- Near the end of the letter:
    - Ask the reader for a specific action
    - Remind the reader of the benefit.
- Create a sense of urgency.
- Make your writing positive and energetic throughout.

- Make your letter visually pleasing and professional.
- Make it easy for your readers to respond to the letter. Include information on how to contact you or when you'll contact them (and make sure you do).
- Consider adding a postscript (P.S.). The postscript is the most-read part of a sales letter. Try a handwritten note to personalize the letter.

IRAC (Issue, Rule, Application, Conclusion) System of Legal Writing

Regardless of whether you must write legal letters, it's useful to know how to use the IRAC system of writing. This technique is used when the need to apply a rule or regulation to a specific situation arises.

The following example shows how to use the IRAC system.[1]

- *Issue*. Did John Kane violate agency ethics regulations when he accepted free tuition to a professional conference on the latest trends in government accounting?
- *Rule*. Ethics Rule 2.1 prohibits acceptance of any gratuity by a government employee from an organization seeking to do business with the government.
- *Application*. John Kane's action involved acceptance of a gratuity. The course tuition had a dollar value of $325, and the conference sponsor was an organization seeking to do business with his agency.
- *Conclusion*. John Kane violated ethics regulations and is therefore subject to discipline.

Letters of Recommendation

Nearly everyone is asked to write a letter of recommendation at one time or another. The following are some guidelines:

1. Review a copy of the candidate's personal statement or application essays so that your letter of recommendation can dovetail with—not conflict with or duplicate—the rest of the application.
2. Ask the applicant for additional information, such as a resume.
3. Give the candidate's full name and the position or other objective the candidate is seeking.
4. Describe your qualifications for comparing the candidate to other candidates:

   "I have personally supervised 10 interns every summer for the past five years in addition to working with more than 200 college graduates in my capacity as training officer for the Recreation Department."

5. Discuss how you know the candidate:

   "I have been Ms. Martin's direct supervisor for the past two years."

6. Choose two or three qualities that you observed in the candidate:

   "Dr. Wood's dedication to his work set a fine example for the entire team. His mentoring and encouragement of new employees will continue to benefit the agency for some time to come."

7. In discussing these qualities, support your statements with specific instances in which the person demonstrated those attributes. Be as concrete and detailed as possible.

   "Donald's thorough knowledge of databases saved us time and money."

8. Compare the candidate's potential with that of peers, if available:

   "Ms. Jones consistently rated in the top 10 percent of her class."

9. Discuss the candidate's potential in his or her chosen field:

   "Because of his intelligence, resourcefulness, and strong interpersonal skills, I enthusiastically recommend Mr. Morales for any intermediate or senior marketing position."

Manager Alert

Do not feel obligated to write a letter of recommendation if you have reservations about the employee's qualifications or character. It is much fairer to everyone involved for you to suggest that someone else might be in a better position to write a recommendation.

Letters Accompanying Reports

When you attach a report, write a brief letter letting the reader know what the report is about. The letter on the following page was sent in 2010 from the executive director of the National Association of Schools of Public Affairs (NASPAA) to OPM Director John Berry.[2]

In this age of instant communication, letters sometimes seem to have lost their importance. However, well-written correspondence reflects well on both you and your organization, improves customer relations, and helps you as a government manager accomplish your goals more easily.

Dear Director Berry,

On behalf of NASPAA's Policy Issues Committee, I am pleased to present our new white paper, "Building the Federal Workforce for the 21st Century: Graduate Students and the Routes of Entry." This paper is the latest in a series of NASPAA efforts to consider and recommend policy options in federal hiring reform for students, based on an examination of the available evidence.

Over the last 18 months, we have appreciated the opportunity to meet with you and your staff to discuss the need for reform in federal student hiring programs, especially the Presidential Management Fellowship. And we applaud the optimism and vision you have shown in bringing sorely needed change to these programs.

We now stand on the threshold of that change.

We look forward to rolling up our sleeves and working with OPM and agencies across government to implement changes to student internship and hiring programs. NASPAA can help create innovative and exciting marketing programs to students and provide needed logistical and academic support for assessment efforts and interviews.

For 32 years, NASPAA has partnered with the federal government to encourage the best graduate students to consider federal careers, and to ensure the road there is a rigorous but supportive one. Let's do it all over again.

Sincerely yours,

Laurel McFarland

NASPAA Executive Director

NOTES

1. Donald G. Rider, *Effective Writing for Feds* (Huntsville, AL: FPMI Communications, 1992).
2. National Association of Schools of Public Affairs. Letter accompanying "Building the Federal Workforce for the 21st Century: Graduate Students and the Routes of Entry." December 23, 2010. Online at www.naspaa.org/PolicyCenter/BerryLetter122310.pdf (accessed January 2013).

Chapter 9

PREPARING REPORTS

A number of tasks in government require preparing reports:

- Preparation of legislation
- Development of policies and procedures
- Staffing
- Program analysis
- Employee evaluation
- Job description
- Budget preparation
- Office design
- Workflow analysis
- Office organization
- Strategic planning
- Annual planning
- Public relations.

A report should be logical, accurate, reliable, and easy to read. Though generally not as conversational as a letter, a report should nonetheless be friendly and professional.

INFORMAL OR BRIEF REPORTS

An informal report might take the form of an email or a written memo. The elements of a good report fall into three categories: introduction, body, and conclusion.

Introduction

The introduction, or opening statement, sets the stage for what will follow. This may be an overview of topics and their significance, a position statement, or conclusions and recommendations. You may also use a combination of these approaches.

Body

The main purpose of the body of a report is to describe or analyze. In *describing,* you attempt to tell a story, such as relating what has happened over the past month or spelling out the steps involved in performing a task. In *analyzing*, you look more closely and make some sense of things, such as providing an explanation of why a problem situation has developed.

Conclusion

The closing of a report is crucial. This is where you convey the thoughts and impressions you want to leave with your reader. The closing may be a concise summary of what you have said, some final recommendations, or actions you plan to take. Like the opening, the closing should be to the point.

FORMAL REPORTS

Formal reports are generally longer than informal reports. The length and complexity of the report often depend upon the length and complexity of the project. Elements of formal reports include some or all of the following:

- Title page
- Any letters relevant to the report
- Executive summary (sometimes called abstract)
- Table of contents
- List of figures (if appropriate)
- List of tables
- List of abbreviations and symbols
- Acknowledgments, preface, or foreword
- Body
    - Purpose of report—subject, scope, plan
    - Background
    - Policy statement
    - Introduction
    - Analysis and supporting data

  - Conclusions
  - Recommendations
- Glossary
- References
- Bibliography
- Appendices
- Index.

Title Page

The title page should include a title indicating the topic and the objective of the report, the writer's name and organization, the person or organization receiving the report, and the date.

Letters

Include any letters authorizing or requesting the report and any letters of transmittal, as applicable.

Executive Summary

Any report of three or more pages must contain a short, informative overview. The executive summary, sometimes called a "management overview," "preliminary summary," or "abstract," is perhaps *the* most important element of the report because it might be the only part that is actually read. It also might be the basis for accepting or rejecting a report for publication or presentation.

The executive summary states (1) the project's background, (2) the purpose and nature of the report, (3) the procedure for the study, (4) budgetary implications, (5) major findings and conclusions, and (6) recommendations. The key to a successful summary is to keep it short (200 to 250 words or less) and informative.

Executive summaries usually appear after the title page and letters (if any). The following executive summary comes from a U.S. Department of Education report[1]:

Higher Education: Gaps in Access and Persistence Study
Executive Summary

Numerous studies, including those of the National Center for Education Statistics (NCES), have documented persistent gaps between the educational attainment of White males and that of Black, Hispanic, American Indian/Alaska Native, and Native Hawaiian/Pacific Islander males. Further, there is evidence of growing gaps by sex within these racial/ethnic groups, as females participate and persist in education at higher rates than their male counterparts. In the interest of formulating policies to address these gaps, Congress directed the U.S. Department of Education to produce a report documenting the gaps in access to and completion of higher education by minority males and to outline specific policies that can help address these gaps (Higher Education Opportunity Act, H.R. 4137, 110th Cong. §1109, 2008). NCES was directed to produce the Higher Education: Gaps in Access and Persistence Study, a statistical report that documents the scope and nature of the gaps by sex and by race/ethnicity.

The primary focus of the Higher Education: Gaps in Access and Persistence Study is to examine gaps in educational participation and attainment between male Blacks, Hispanics, Native Hawaiians/Pacific Islanders, and American Indians/Alaska Natives and their female counterparts and to examine gaps between males in these racial/ethnic groups and White males. The secondary focus of the report is to examine overall sex and racial/ethnic differences. In addition to these descriptive indicators, this report also includes descriptive multivariate analyses of variables that are associated with male and female postsecondary attendance and attainment.

Postsecondary attendance rates are generally lower for youth from lower socioeconomic backgrounds and those from various racial/ethnic groups (e.g., Blacks and Hispanics) when compared to Whites and Asians (Aud et al. 2011). In 2010, as in every year since 1980, a lower percentage of male than female 18- to 24-year-olds were enrolled either in college or graduate school (39 vs. 47 percent). This pattern was also observed for Whites (43 vs. 51 percent), Blacks (31 vs. 43 percent), Hispanics (26 vs. 36 percent), American Indians (24 vs. 33 percent), and persons of two or more races (40 vs. 49 percent). In addition to college enrollment differences, there are gaps in postsecondary attainment for males and females. For instance, among first-time students seeking bachelor's degrees who started full time at a 4-year college in 2004, a higher percentage of females than males completed bachelor's degrees within 6 years (61 vs. 56 percent)—a pattern that held across all racial/ethnic groups.

This report will document the scope and nature of a number of differences between sex and racial/ethnic groups in education preparation and achievement as well as differences in postsecondary access, persistence, and attainment between males and females within and across racial/ethnic groups. The report presents indicators that include the most recently available, nationally representative data from NCES, other federal agencies, and selected items from the ACT and the College Board. The report draws on multiple sources that represent different years and different populations.

Table of Contents

A well-organized, detailed table of contents makes it easy for the reader to identify all the elements in a document. The table of contents should indicate the headings in the report, along with their page numbers. It also should include all items in the report (except itself and the title page).

List of Figures

A list of figures can be included in reports with more than five illustrations (drawings, photographs, maps, charts, and graphs). The list of figures is a separate table of contents for the illustrations, which are numbered consecutively with Arabic numbers.

List of Tables

A report with more than five tables can also contain a list of tables. This list is a separate table of contents for the tables, which are numbered consecutively with Arabic numbers.

List of Abbreviations and Acronyms

This list is useful if a report contains many abbreviations and acronyms. List each abbreviation and acronym in alphabetical order and note what it stands for.

Acknowledgments, Preface, and Foreword

Acknowledgments are an author's expression of gratitude to all who helped with the report. They usually include editors, proofreaders, advisors, and anyone who provided support or inspiration. The *preface*, which is written by the author, addresses the purpose, limitations, and scope of the report; it may also include acknowledgments if there is not a separate section for them. The *foreword* is written by someone other than the author or editor, usually someone eminent, and is included to lend credibility to the report.

Body

The body, which is the main part of the report, provides a complete account of the topic. It should cover both technical details and managerial implications.

The following are included in the body:

- *Purpose*. This briefly presents the subject, scope, and organizational plan of the report.
- *Background.* This part of the report tells the reader how the report came to be written—the problems that led to it, the need for clarification of a subject, etc.
- *Policy statement.* If the report results from a specific public policy, that should be spelled out here.
- *Introduction.* The introduction deals with the subject of the report, leading into the text.
- *Analysis and supporting data.* Introduce only enough data to prove each issue. To be authoritative, be as concrete and specific as possible. Use numbers and percentages, quotes or opinions from respected sources, and tables and graphs.
- *Conclusions.* Your conclusions must prove your position by summarizing the implications of the data:
    - Does the analysis show that the conclusions are correct?
    - Are there factors that could affect the validity of the conclusions?
- *Recommendations*. Finally, tell readers what they are expected to do to put your position into effect and what you, the writer, will do to further your position.

Glossary

The glossary is an alphabetical listing of technical terms and their definitions, written in dictionary style. The terms selected will depend on the intended readers' background.

References

Any materials referred to or quoted from should be listed in a references section. References may take the form of footnotes or endnotes. In general, longer reports should include references at the end of each section of the report.

Bibliography

The bibliography is a separate listing of all source materials used in researching the report but not necessarily cited in the text itself.

Appendices

Appendices contain information that supports or clarifies the report but is too detailed or voluminous to appear in the text without impeding the flow of ideas. This information might take the form of questionnaires or interviews used in the study; tabular results of the questionnaires and interviews; other data, presented in charts, graphs, and tables; and correspondence.

Appendices are especially useful when your report is going to a diverse audience, some of whom may not want or need to read the information in the appendix.

Index

The index is an alphabetical, cross-referenced list of all topics and subjects of importance in the report.

FORMATS FOR GOVERNMENT REPORTS

Different formats may be appropriate for different types of government reports.

Research Reports

Managers are often required to review research reports. A research report is the final product of an involved process of investigation, critical thinking, source evaluation, organization, and composition. Information can come from secondary research, which is research conducted previously for another purpose, or from primary research, which is new research conducted specifically for the current project. Information also can come from internal or external sources.

Internal sources include

- Management information systems
- Personnel files, especially reports
- Budgets
- Expense records
- Travel records
- Timesheets
- Correspondence files
- Retirement, insurance, and Social Security records
- Minutes of meetings
- Intranet information

External sources include

- Reports by other federal, state, and local agencies
- Reports from industry, trade journals, and corporate yearly statements
- Reports and files of community service organizations, such as the Chamber of Commerce, charitable organizations, unions, fraternal organizations, foundations, and political parties

- Newspaper and magazine files
- University and college faculty studies
- Libraries
- Public records of marriage, health, parentage, age, welfare, place of business, property ownership and use, and taxation
- Census Bureau records
- Sales and inventory records
- Internet sites.

MANAGER ALERT

Any research effort in the government is affected by the politics of the situation. Researchers need to take special care to conduct their work objectively. If there is disagreement over conclusions, these should be handled with both confidence and respect.

White Papers

The term *white paper* originated in the early 20th century in England. A white paper, or *command paper*, referred to a parliamentary report, bound in a white cover, that laid out a government policy or proposed action. Today, white papers are generally defined as communication tools used to explain something complex to an audience with little or no background on the topic.

Most white papers are now found on the Internet; regardless of their source, they provide information and analysis regarding an issue readers are facing.

As a government manager, you or your staff might write a white paper for a number of reasons:

- To educate the public or an official on a complex subject
- To educate the media by providing the basis of an article
- To provide credibility on a given topic
- To redefine the way people view a given subject
- To answer a pressing question
- To explain a trend.

The components of a white paper are the opening, the body, and the closing. In the opening, you state your purpose. In the body, you give (1) the benefits of dealing with the issue, (2) critical background information, (3) key considerations regarding your solution if you offer one, and (4) supporting evidence. In the closing you restate your purpose.

Business Strategy Reports

A business strategy report, or proposal, is a document that attempts to persuade the reader to follow a plan or course of action. Although business strategy reports can be internal or external, they are almost always internal in the government.

A business strategy report proposes to others in the organization a change or improvement. Quite often, such proposals seek approval for a capital expenditure; therefore, persuasion is a primary purpose of these documents.

Typically, business strategy reports take the form of a memo and contain the following information:

- *Background leading to the problem.* You start off by describing how the problem developed, its effects, and any efforts made to solve it.
- *Proposal for fixing the problem.*
- *Arguments in favor of the proposed solution.* In this section you describe the benefits for your reader, using supporting evidence. These might include any of the following:
    - Results of experiments
    - Definitions
    - Comparisons
    - Required equipment, materials, and personnel
    - Quotes
    - Proposed schedule
    - Expert testimony
    - Statistics
    - Reasons
    - Examples.
- *Opposing arguments and rebuttals.* You can understand and address opposing arguments through research, discussion, and feedback. Ask a person who is opposed to your proposal to give his or her viewpoint. Then think of ways to refute the arguments.
- *Request for action.* Let your readers know clearly what steps they need to take.
- *Conclusion.* Restate recommendations and offer other information or assistance.

Feasibility Reports

A feasibility report explores the chances of success for a particular project, venture, or commitment. While a business strategy report usually recommends one solution, a feasibility report evaluates two or more possible solutions. The subject of such a report might be a move, the development of a new product or service, an expansion, or a major purchase. The feasibility report examines and compares alternatives, analyzes the pros and cons, and suggests which, if any, of the alternatives are feasible. It includes the following information:

- Statement of purpose
- Statement of problem
- Scope
- Alternatives under consideration
- Conclusion
- Recommendations.

Critical Incident Reports

Critical incident reports deal with occurrences that interfere with normal activity, such as accidents, equipment failures, communication breakdowns, unplanned work stoppages, and damage from fire, flood, or storms. These reports enable managers to determine the cause of a problem and to make the changes necessary to prevent its recurrence. Typically, critical incident reports use a memo format and contain the following information:

- Description of the problem (who, what, when, where, why, and how)
- Resulting injuries or deaths
- Resulting damage
- Costs (in terms of lost work, equipment damage, worker's compensation awards, or lawsuits)
- Witnesses
- Any action taken (including treatment of injuries)
- Recommendations (such as training, equipment improvements, or protective clothing).

Because critical incident reports might be used as evidence in lawsuits, it is important to:

- Include precise times, dates, locations, treatment of injuries, names of witnesses, and any other crucial information
- Avoid making statements of condemnation or blame

- Avoid making definite statements about the cause
- Respect the need for confidentiality.

Statements of Work

A statement of work (SOW) is the written description of an agency requirement; it is typically used in the acquisition of supplies or services. Development of an SOW is considered the most important step in the procurement process. The SOW shapes the invitation for bid or request for proposals. During the solicitation process, contractors use the SOW to develop and price their proposals. Then the government uses the SOW to evaluate proposals. After contract award, the SOW forms the basis for assessing contract performance.[2]

The SOW is a legally binding agreement supporting the conditions of the contract. Therefore, it should be clear, precise, and to the point. It's a good idea to ask someone from the legal department to review the SOW to avoid contradictions, redundancies, and misunderstandings.

Although there is no single correct way to write a SOW, the following format can be used within any government agency:[3]

1. *Introduction and Scope Statement.* The introduction should accurately reflect the agency's requirements. It should include background information, including the rationale for the project; any pertinent historical information; an explanation of how the project relates to the overall program and to other projects or studies; and any problems of which the contractor should be aware.
2. *Requirements.* This is the most important part of the SOW. The requirements should be realistic, definite, and nonrestrictive. They should explain what the government wants, when the products or services are due, and what criteria will be used to determine whether requirements were met. They should also include any special considerations or restraints that apply.
3. *References.* The references section supports the requirements cited elsewhere in the SOW. When citing documents, be careful to reference only the pertinent sections. Also, check to make sure that there are no conflicts between the SOW and any of the documents cited.
4. *Delivery.* Clearly specify when, where, and how the products and services are to be delivered.
5. *Progress and Compliance.* In this section, list any interim and final reports due, note inspection procedures, and explain how the government and the contractor will know when the project requirements are satisfied.
6. *Notes and Other Information.* This section includes any information or attachments not given in the other part of the SOW, such as technical drawings or a list of personnel qualifications.

The following guidelines can help in crafting a clear, useful SOW:[4]

- *Avoid ambiguities or inconsistencies in requirements*. These can crop up if the requirements are spread throughout the SOW instead of being concentrated in the technical requirements section.
- *Describe each requirement fully and explicitly*. Do not depend on the contractor's intuitive understanding.
- *Use the word shall to express an action by the contractor*. The SOW contains what are essentially commands to the contractor. Using the imperative ensures that there is no misunderstanding of the contractor's responsibilities. Use the word *will* to express an action by the government. Do not use *will* in conjunction with contractor actions because the word does not expressly require the contractor to take action. The consistent use of *shall* for contractor actions and *will* for government actions makes it easier to distinguish contractor responsibilities from government responsibilities.
- *Avoid vague words and phrases*, such as *similar, type, average, about, high quality, as required, as applicable, as necessary, best effort, best practice, insofar as possible, may include, but not limited to*, and *etc.* These words cause confusion and make evaluation of performance more difficult.
- When referring to other parts of the SOW or to other documents, *explicitly cite the page or paragraph number of the item*.

Every week government managers are typically involved in some phase of the study/report process. Some volunteer; others are summoned to the task. Knowing the correct formats and guidelines for various types of reports can make your job as a manager easier and more effective.

NOTES

1. National Center for Education Statistics, U.S. Department of Education. "Higher Education: Gaps in Access and Persistence Study." August 2012. Online at http://nces.ed.gov/pubs2012/2012046/commissioner.asp (accessed January 2013).
2. Judson Monroe, *Effective Research and Report Writing in Government* (New York: McGraw-Hill, 1980), 6–7.
3. Peter S. Cole, and Michael G. Martin. *How to Write a Statement of Work, sixth edition* (Tysons Corner, VA: Management Concepts Press, 2012), 5.
4. Michael G. Martin, *Federal Statements of Work: A Practical Guide* (Vienna, VA. Management Concepts, 2008), 25–37.

Chapter 10

OTHER FORMS OF GOVERNMENT WORKPLACE WRITING

Writing in today's government workplace requires a wide variety of skills, including collaborating, ghostwriting, and preparing talking points. A government manager also needs to be adept in a wide range of areas, including performance appraisals, budget justifications, policies, and regulations. Flexibility and the willingness to tackle a variety of different tasks are key.

COLLABORATIVE WRITING

Collaborative writing occurs whenever two or more people are involved in writing or approving a document. Most government workplace writing is collaborative writing. Even if one person writes the first draft independently, it will likely go through many technical experts, managers, editors, and subject matter experts before it is released. Anyone involved in the writing process must know how to work with others—how to plan, organize, and give and take suggestions.

When several team members are working on the same document, they can save time by using software tools:

- Use the "track changes" feature to strike through or add text in a contrasting color without destroying the original text.
- Select a split screen to display the original and the edited version with the changes highlighted.

Manager Alert

When you are managing a writing team, make sure all members understand who will draft, edit, and sign off on which sections of the document. If team members can't agree, you may need to assign these tasks.

Make sure team members understand the purpose, subject, and audience of the document.

Help the team develop a production schedule or milestone chart with realistic deadlines and time built in for the unexpected.

If more than one person is writing the document, make sure that it is divided into manageable chunks and assigned accordingly. One of the editor's jobs is to make the document sounds as if one person wrote it.

Encourage reviewers to provide constructive comments, and help writers to accept the comments in the right spirit.

Help the team work out any frustrations and problems that may arise.

GHOSTWRITING

As a government manager you might be asked to write a letter for someone else's signature or prepare a report or speech for an upper-level manager. Or, you might ask others to do the same for you. Understanding the realities of ghostwriting can help you and your collaborator complete the project successfully.

Delegating the Task

Make sure you delegate the writing task to someone who understands the situation well enough to take on the job, and then make sure that you work closely with that person, especially if he or she has little experience writing. Make sure you're clear about exactly what you want and that you communicate your expectations to the writer.

Don't expect the writer to duplicate your style; instead, add some of your own personal touches before signing off on the document.

Taking on the Task

If you are the one asked to write the letter, speech, or report, make sure you understand the task as thoroughly as possible. Ask questions, become informed, and consider this a learning opportunity. If the document is long, write one section and get feedback from the person who asked you to write before going on to the rest. You should expect changes, even though the draft represents your best effort.

TALKING POINTS

Talking points are lists of key ideas and facts to help speakers provide clear, accurate information. They are intended to keep speakers on track, but not to be read word for word. Managers are sometimes asked to write talking points for others, or they may write them for their own presentations. An organization can increase its effectiveness by "speaking with one voice"—using shared talking points to respond to inquiries, especially during a crisis.

Here are some guidelines for writing talking points:

- Understand the purpose of the presentation.
- Know the audience and how much time is allotted for the presentation.
- Research the topic thoroughly and make sure you have accurate information.
- Create a short list of bulleted ideas. Keep the points concise.
- Since talking points are often sensitive, do not provide them to the press.
- If it would be helpful, pair your talking points with a fact sheet.
- In the first bullet point, state the facts of the situation—who, what, where, when, why, and how. In the following bullet points, provide more detailed information on the topic.
- If the talking points are in response to an adverse event, give positive information but do not hide or understate the negatives.
- In the final bullet point, focus on the message you want to leave with the listeners.

POSITION DESCRIPTIONS

A position description documents the major duties, responsibilities, and organizational relationships of a job. Because it serves as the official record of the classification of the job and is used to make many personnel decisions, it should be written in clear, concise, and easy-to-understand language. The description of each position must be kept up-to-date and include information about the job that is significant to its classification.

Each agency determines who will prepare position descriptions. Depending on particular circumstances within an organization, the position description may be written by the employee in the job, the supervisor or manager, a personnel specialist, or any combination of these.

Position descriptions are written in one of two basic formats: narrative or factor evaluation system (FES). Most new standards are issued in FES, and many agencies have decided to prepare all position descriptions following the FES factor format.

Manager Alert

Regardless of the format, have the immediate supervisor read and sign the position description, certifying its accuracy.

Narrative Position Descriptions

A narrative description generally includes four different kinds of information:

1. *Introduction*—a statement of the primary purpose of the position and its relationship to the organization
2. *Major Duties and Responsibilities*—a statement of the important, regular, and recurring duties and responsibilities assigned to the position
3. *Controls over the Position*—a statement of how the work is assigned, the kind of supervision and guidance received, and the kind of review given to work in process or upon completion
4. *Special Qualification Requirements*—a statement of any valid knowledge, skill, education, certification, etc., required by the position if it is not readily apparent from reading the description, such as foreign language proficiency or licensure.

A good description is one that is a forthright presentation of the work assigned to a position. Statements of duties are often clearest when they include a strong action verb and a noun that together define a duty or task. Describe the work performed rather than detailing names, places, dates, etc. Such information only makes the position description become outdated faster.

FES Position Descriptions

FES includes nine factors common to most nonsupervisory positions in general schedule (GS) occupations. Several of these factors have two or more subfactors or concepts that together represent the intent of the overall factor. The FES factors and their subfactors are as follows:

Factor 1—Knowledge Required by the Position

- Kind or nature of knowledge and skills needed
- How the knowledge and skills are used in doing the work

Factor 2—Supervisory Controls

- How the work is assigned
- Employee's responsibility for carrying out the work
- How the work is reviewed

Factor 3—Guidelines

- Nature of guidelines for performing the work
- Judgment needed to apply the guidelines or develop new guidelines

Factor 4—Complexity

- Nature of the assignment
- Difficulty involved in identifying what needs to be done
- Difficulty and originality involved in performing the work

Factor 5—Scope and Effect

- Purpose of the work
- Impact of the work product or service

Factor 6—Personal Contacts

- People and conditions/setting under which contacts are made

Factor 7—Purpose of Contacts

- Reasons for contacts in Factor 6

(In some FES standards, the point values for factors 6 and 7 are combined into a matrix chart. The levels of each factor are described separately.)

Factor 8—Physical Demands

- Nature, frequency, and intensity of physical activity

Factor 9—Work Environment

- Risks and discomforts caused by physical surroundings and the safety precautions necessary to avoid accidents or discomfort.

Basic Terms

The following are definitions of basic terms relating to position classification standards:

1. *General Schedule*—The broadest subdivision of the classification system covered by U.S. Code Title 5, Government Organization and Employees. It includes a range of levels of difficulty and responsibility for covered positions from grades GS–1 to GS–15. It is designated by "GS" for supervisory and nonsupervisory positions at all of these grade levels. (Most positions above grade GS–15 are included in the Senior Executive Service, which is outside the General Schedule.)
2. *Occupational Group*—A major subdivision of the General Schedule, comprising associated or related occupations (e.g., the Accounting and

Budget Group, GS–500; the Engineering and Architecture Group, GS–800; the General Administrative, Clerical, and Office Services Group, GS–300).

3. *Series*—A subdivision of an occupational group consisting of positions similar in terms of specialized line of work and qualification requirements. Series are designated by a title and number (e.g., the Accounting Series, GS–510; the Secretary Series, GS–318; the Microbiology Series, GS–403).
4. *Grade*—The numerical designation, GS–1 through GS–15, that identifies the range of difficulty and responsibility and the level of qualification requirements of positions included in the General Schedule.
5. *Class of Positions*—All positions that are classified to the same schedule, series, and grade and are sufficiently alike to warrant like treatment in personnel processes such as testing, selection, transfer, and promotion.
6. *Position*—The duties and responsibilities that make up the work performed by an employee.
7. *Position Description*—The official description of management's assignment of duties, responsibilities, and supervisory relationships to a position.
8. *Classification Standard*—Issued by OPM to relate the grade level definitions in Title 5 to specific work situations and thereby provide the basis for assigning each position the appropriate title, series, and grade.[1]

PERFORMANCE REVIEWS

Providing written and oral feedback to employees regarding their performance is an important role for government managers. OPM has outlined the following eight steps for managers to follow in developing performance plans:

Step 1: Look at the overall picture. Review the agency's strategic plan and annual performance plan to see which performance goals and performance measures are already in place.

Step 2: Determine work unit accomplishments. Use one or more of the following methods:

- *Cascading*: Tie the agency's goals to the work unit level. Then determine which of the work unit's accomplishments directly affect the organization's goals.
- *Customer-focused:* Determine which products or services customers expect from the work unit.
- *Work flow charting:* A work flow chart is a picture of the major steps in a work process or project.

Step 3: Determine individual accomplishments that support work unit goals. List what the unit member must produce or perform to support work unit goals.

Step 4: Convert expected accomplishments into performance elements, including type and priority. First, decide which accomplishments should be included as elements in the performance plan. Next, classify the elements (critical, noncritical, etc.). Then assign weights or priorities to each element.

Step 5: Determine work unit and individual measures. Include both general and specific measures.

Step 6: Develop work unit and individual standards. To develop the standards, first determine the number of levels your appraisal program uses and what level an employee must meet to be retained in a job.

Step 7: Determine how to monitor performance. This includes (1) what data to collect for each performance element, (2) the source of the data, (3) whether to collect all the data or just a sample, (4) when to collect the data, and (5) who will collect the data and who will receive it.

Review existing reports and feedback tables or graphs where necessary or applicable. Try to design a feedback process that gives feedback automatically. The performance review should emphasize and clarify job requirements, give employees feedback on their achievements in fulfilling those requirements, and help them continually improve.

To achieve these goals, the feedback should following these guidelines:

- *Specificity.* Tangible, objective, and powerful feedback relates to a specific goal. Instead of just telling employees they are "doing a good job," tell them they are doing well because they exceeded their goal by 10 percent. Instead of "Your work has been sloppy lately," state that the last report contained three statistical errors.
- *Timeliness.* Confront any performance problems right away. If employees have reached or exceeded their goal, give them positive reinforcement as soon as possible.
- *Manner.* Try to present accurate, factual, and complete feedback, delivered in as positive a manner as possible. The tone of the review should be objective and unbiased, the language nonjudgmental, and the emphasis on resolution of any problems.

Step 8: Check the performance plan. Use the following checklist as a tool for reviewing the performance plan you have developed:

- Are the critical elements truly critical? Does failure on the critical element mean that the employee's overall performance is unacceptable?
- Is the range of acceptable performance clear? Are the performance expectations quantifiable, observable, and verifiable?
- Are the standards attainable? Are expectations reasonable?

- Are the standards challenging? Does the work unit or employee need to exert a reasonable amount of effort to reach the "fully successful" performance level?
- Are the standards fair? Are they comparable to expectations for other employees in similar positions? Do they allow for some margin of error?
- Are the standards applicable? Can the appraiser use the standards to appraise performance? Can the appraiser manage the data collected through the measurement process?
- Will work units and employees understand what is required?
- Are the elements and standards flexible? Can they be adapted readily to changes in resources or objectives?
- If your program permits appraising elements at levels above the fully successful or equivalent level, is the fully successful or equivalent standard surpassable? Is it possible for a work unit's or an employee's performance to exceed it?[2]

Manager Alert

The Merit Systems Protection Board offers recommendations for agencies in writing retention standards in order to avoid litigation.

- In almost all cases, the standard should allow for some error; it should not be "impermissibly absolute." You should describe the regularity of the occurrence of the task required, but avoid the requirement to do it "always." Ask yourself the following questions:
    - How many times may the employee fail this requirement and still be acceptable?
    - Does the retention standard use words such as "all," "never," or "each"? These words may alert you to problems.
    - If the retention standard allows no errors, would a single breach result in loss of life, injury, breach of national security, or great monetary loss? Only in such cases is an absolute standard acceptable.
- Make sure your standard expresses the level of work the supervisor wants to see. It should not describe negative performance or a "backward" standard. Examples of backward standards are "Completes fewer than four products a year" or "Performs work inaccurately."

Each critical element must have a fully successful or equivalent standard, and it is recommended, though not required, that non-critical and additional elements have such a standard.

BUDGET JUSTIFICATIONS

Competition for government resources is intense and requires careful planning and preparation of budget requests. Writing skill could be the competitive edge that makes your budget request succeed next year.

The primary purpose of a written budget is to give friendly legislators the ammunition they need to argue your case and to justify their votes to their constituency. As a government manager, you need to direct your justification to several different audiences:

- OMB examiners
- Agency budget staff
- Legislators and legislative staffers
- Lobbyists.

Federal employees should be familiar with OMB Circular A-11, which provides technical policy guidance regarding the format and content of budgets submitted to OMB. This document is issued annually on OMB's website, www.whitehouse.gov/OMB.

In addition to the guidance provided by OMB, each agency issues formal and informal guidance regarding budget requests. A government manager involved in writing budget requests should follow carefully the directions contained in agency call letters or other documents governing budget submissions.

Since 2005 federal agencies have been required to submit a performance budget. They must show how funding will help the agency achieve short- and long-term goals in pursuit of its mission. The budget must link the agency's mission, strategic goals, programs, and long-term as well as annual performance goals.

Effective budget justifications usually describe events that are intended to occur within a year or more. Their time frame is the end of the budget year (September 30) unless a different time frame is stated. The budget justification describes intended outcomes, not hoped-for outcomes. These outcomes are within the agency's jurisdiction, program authority, and power.

Before you begin writing a budget justification, make sure you have reviewed and analyzed the following information:

- Agency mission, strategic goals, and annual performance goals
- Means and strategies for achieving those goals
- Description of agency, legislative authority, and appropriations language
- For each activity:
    - Statement of functions and purpose

- o Description of changes requested for the budget year as compared to the current year
- o Productivity increase and management improvements
- o Summary of budget approved by OMB
- o Historical tables:
  - – Program costs linked to appropriations
  - – Employment by organization unit
  - – Obligations or costs by object class
  - – Summary of workload indicators.

As you organize the justification information, make sure you include goals, objectives, workloads, accomplishments, beneficiaries served, and funding needs.

> **Manager Alert**
>
> The budget justification should show clearly the cause-and-effect relationship between the funding and the achievement of the outcome or objective.

EXHIBIT 300 REPORTS

A supplement to Circular A-11, *The Capital Programming Guide*, addresses the need for effective program and project management. The guide focuses on an important document, Exhibit 300 (E-300).

Major acquisitions and investments across the federal government must be reported through the E-300. The E-300 is a business case that forms one element of an agency's budget submission. The exhibit allows agency leadership and OMB to compare different projects using a common format and rating criteria. Exhibit 300 asks for information about project planning, staffing, risk management, lifecycle management, acquisition, earned value, and more; it can thus serve as a valuable communication tool.

The document provides an opportunity for the project team and agency leadership to demonstrate to OMB that the disciplines of good project management are in place on every major project. On the other hand, if a project suffers from one of the following, it could very well be removed from the budget submission:

- The project has not made significant progress in resolving Federal Information Security Management Act security requirements.

- The project is seriously over budget.
- The project is seriously behind schedule.
- The project fails to provide the basic functionality identified in the requirements analysis.
- A qualified and experienced project manager is not in charge of the investment.
- The project is no longer a priority for the agency mission and budget.

Accordingly, government managers should prepare the E-300 document carefully and thoroughly.

POLICIES

A policy is a statement of principles or guidelines that helps organizations enforce rules consistently.

Sometimes managers are asked to help formulate policy for their agency. They may offer input or actually have a hand in writing the policies. Carefully written employment policies provide the structure within which an organization governs its employee relations. Sound policies can serve as both an effective communication device and a legal protection. A policies and procedures manual lets managers and employees know what is expected and prevents misunderstandings. Also, supervisors and managers are more likely to apply policies consistently when the policies are clearly communicated in writing. Finally, well-written policies show commitment to a positive work environment and to fair employment practices.

How Policies Are Developed

Policies reflect the views of the organization as a whole in a given area. Their authority usually comes from prior consensus—formal or informal. The following are the most common ways in which policies are created or modified:

- Documenting a practice that is already in place or is simple enough that consensus can be reached easily. For example, an organization might formalize a policy regarding employee gift-giving that has already become established.
- Proposing a policy for review and consideration by the organization. This might follow a sudden change, such as the bombing of the World Trade Center, which led to the adoption of policies regarding security.
- Creating or modifying policy to clarify an area that is unclear or that has gradually become a problem. After employees gained access to the Internet in the 1990s, some employees began to spend too much time on non–work-related websites or on personal email. As a result, organizations began to write policies governing Internet access.

- Although written policies in general are not legally required, certain policies might be needed to help establish good-faith compliance with federal and state law. For example, the Supreme Court has indicated that employers may protect themselves against liability for sexual harassment by having clearly articulated policies against sexual harassment that include effective complaint procedures.

Guidelines for Writing Policies

The following guidelines can help government managers in writing clear, effective policies:

- Avoid imposing policies from the top down. Try to work with what is already good practice within your organization or work group.
- Consult widely. Talk to people within your organization. Make a special effort to engage potential critics of the new policy. Also, see what policies are working well for other organizations and adopt them for your own if they fit.
- Keep policies general so that they can be implemented easily. Avoid precise rules that try to cover every situation that might arise. Try to avoid all-inclusive lists such as work rules.
- Steer clear of any promises that could be interpreted as a contract. For example, don't state that the organization will "only" or "always" do something or "must" act in a particular way.
- Give appropriate examples to illustrate your policies. A well-chosen example can often make things far clearer than a long, detailed description.
- Provide plenty of time for discussion. Allow people time to think about the new guidelines. You don't want them to feel that you are pushing a new policy through to avoid discussion.

Components of a Policy

In writing a policy, include the following information[3]:

- State your purpose. "This document provides general recommended policy, or a model, for assisting agencies or departments in defining acceptable use conditions for Executive Branch employee personal use of Government office equipment including information technology."
- Give any background (general principles, etc.) needed to further clarify the purpose of the policy. "Taxpayers have the right to depend on their Government to manage their tax dollars wisely and effectively. . . . Executive Branch employees should be provided with a professional supportive work environment. They should be given the tools needed to effectively carry out their assigned responsibilities."

- Identify the authority for the policy. "Authority for this policy is cited as 5 U.S.C. sec 301 which provides that the head of an executive department or military department may prescribe regulations for the use of its property; and Executive Order 13011, Federal Information Technology, section 3(a)(1), which delineates the responsibilities of the Chief Information Office (CIO) Council in providing recommendations to agency heads relating to the management and use of information technology resources."
- Identify to whom the policy applies. "Agency officials may apply this policy to contractor personnel, interns, and other non-government employees through incorporation by reference in contracts or memorandums of agreement as conditions for using Government office equipment and space."
- Give the date when the policy goes into effect. "This model makes use of material already implemented in various agencies or departments' personal use policies and can be implemented [immediately] unless superseded by any other applicable law or regulation. . . ."
- Provide any definitions needed to clarify the policy. "Personal use means any activity that is conducted for purposes other than accomplishing official or otherwise authorized activity."
- Establish the standards for the policy. "Misuse or inappropriate personal use of government equipment includes . . . the creation, copying, transmission, or retransmission of chain letters or other unauthorized mass mailings regardless of subject matter."

Manager Alert

Standards should be measurable in terms of quality, quantity, or time.

The following is a sample policy on workplace violence issued by OPM[4]:

Sample Written Policy Statement

MEMORANDUM FOR EMPLOYEES OF THE DEPARTMENT OF ___________

FROM: DEPARTMENT OR AGENCY HEAD

SUBJECT: Workplace Violence

It is the [*insert Department or Agency name*]'s policy to promote a safe environment for its employees. The Department is committed to working with its employees to maintain a work environment free from violence, threats of violence, harassment, intimidation, and other disruptive behavior. While this kind of conduct is not pervasive at our agency, no agency is immune. Every agency will be affected by disruptive behavior at one time or another.

Violence, threats, harassment, intimidation, and other disruptive behavior in our workplace will not be tolerated; that is, all reports of incidents will be taken seriously and will be dealt with appropriately. Such behavior can include oral or written statements, gestures, or expressions that communicate a direct or indirect threat of physical harm. Individuals who commit such acts may be removed from the premises and may be subject to disciplinary action, criminal penalties, or both.

We need your cooperation to implement this policy effectively and maintain a safe working environment. Do not ignore violent, threatening, harassing, intimidating, or other disruptive behavior. If you observe or experience such behavior by anyone on agency premises, whether he or she is an agency employee or not, report it immediately to a supervisor or manager. Supervisors and managers who receive such reports should seek advice from the Employee Relations Office at xxx-xxxx regarding investigating the incident and initiating appropriate action. **[PLEASE NOTE: Threats or assaults that require immediate attention by security or police should be reported first to security at xxx-xxxx or to police at 911.]**

I will support all efforts made by supervisors and agency specialists in dealing with violent, threatening, harassing, intimidating or other disruptive behavior in our workplace and will monitor whether this policy is being implemented effectively. If you have any questions about this policy statement, please contact ___________ at xxx-xxxx.

REGULATIONS

A regulation is an official rule, law, or order stating what may or may not be done or how something must be done; issued by a government department or agency, it has the force of law. Government agencies at all levels—federal, state, and local—are working to word regulations in plain language. The Office of the Federal Register, National Archives and Records Administration, provides a guide to legal writing at www.archives.gov/federal-register/write/legal-docs.

The types of writing described in this chapter and the previous one touch on only some of the responsibilities of federal managers. Managers also may respond to requests by Congress for specific information, answer questions from Inspectors General regarding possible misconduct, assist in preparing performance and accountability reports, provide data to the public or the press, and contribute new ideas through blogging. These forms of writing require varying information and diverse styles. However, the basic principles of correctness, clarity, precision, conciseness, and professionalism apply to all forms of writing.

NOTES

1. For more information, see U.S. Office of Personnel Management, *The Classifier's Handbook*, TS-107, August 1991. Online at www.opm.gov/fedclass/clashnbk.pdf (accessed January 2013).
2. U.S. Office of Personnel Management, *A Handbook for Measuring Employee Performance,* September 2011. Online at www.opm.gov/perform/wppdf/handbook.pdf (accessed January 2013).
3. Chief Information Office Council of the General Services Administration, *Recommended Executive Branch Model Policy/Guidance on Limited Personal Use of Government Office Equipment Including Information Technology*. Online at www.govexec.com (accessed January 2013).
4. U.S. Office of Personnel Management, *Dealing with Workplace Violence: A Guide for Agency Planner.*
5. Part I: Section 2, Development of Written Policy Statement. Online at www.opm.gov/Employment_and_Benefits/WorkLife/OfficialDocuments/handbooksguides/WorkplaceViolence/p1-s2.asp (accessed January 2013).

Chapter 11

USING SOCIAL MEDIA

Government agencies, in response to public demand, are making greater use of social media to improve transparency, collaboration, and participation. Social media tools present unparalleled opportunities for collaborative government—but implementing these tools comes with unique challenges. It is important for managers to become familiar with relevant policies and guidelines as well as to take advantage of the many good examples across government so that they can implement these tools.

Social media refers to interactive communication based on the Internet and mobile technologies. In this form of communication, the audience is no longer a passive recipient of messages but an active participant in the conversation. Social media changes the method and content of communication among agencies, organizations, communities, and individuals. The social media explosion has been made possible by the development of "Web 2.0," which describes the changing trends in the use of web technology and design to enhance creativity, communications, secure information-sharing, collaboration, and web functionality.

In response to the increased use of social media, agencies are issuing policies and guidelines for government employees and contractors. The guidelines apply to all employees who participate in social media platforms. Some of the more commonly used platforms are the following:

- Social networking sites (Facebook, Google+, Linkedin)
- Microblogging sites (Twitter, Tumblr, Flipr)
- Blogs (including agency official business and personal blogs, as well as comments)
- Video and photo sharing websites (Flickr, YouTube, SmugMug, Snapfish)
- Forums and discussion boards (Google Groups, Yahoo! Groups)
- Online information repositories/encyclopedias (Wikipedia, MAX).

Agencies encourage the use of social media in support of their individual missions. However, in recognition of security and other threats, they are developing policies and guidelines to help employees and contractors understand what is—and is not—appropriate and how to properly use and protect government equipment.

POLICY REGARDING SOCIAL MEDIA

Government policy generally applies to two levels of social media engagement:

- Official use—social media engagement on behalf of the agency on sites where the agency has an official web presence
- Personal use—day-to-day use of social media sites by agency users, not related to official duties.

In December 2012, the U.S. Office of Personnel Management (OPM) published its policy and guidelines regarding the use of social media. OPM's policy states that "Agency users must be mindful that in their personal participation in social media sites, they must not hold themselves out as presenting the official position of OPM, except with the express permission of the Office of Communications and Public Liaison (CPL). Further, Agency users must comply with the Policy on Personal Use of Government Office Equipment and other applicable policies and procedures. Finally, agency users must be aware that misconduct committed on a social media site may result in appropriate discipline."[1]

OPM requires that agency program officials obtain review and approval from the CPL and the Office of the Chief Information Officer before implementing any social media site on behalf of the agency. Personnel must obtain supervisory approval prior to creating or contributing significant content to external social media sites or engaging in recurring exchanges with the public.

Like other agencies, OPM posts disclaimer language on its web page as well as on any third-party media site or tool used by the agency. The disclaimer warns that activity on third-party websites is governed by the security and privacy policies of those sites and notifies users that the agency does not control, modify, or endorse comments or opinions provided by visitors to the site.[2]

Federal employees are also subject to the following:

- Standards of Conduct for Employees of the Executive Branch (5 C.F.R. Part 2635)
- The Hatch Act (5 U.S.C. 7321-7326), which governs partisan political activity of executive branch employees. Personnel are encouraged to review the Office of Special Counsel's "Frequently Asked Questions Regarding Social Media and the Hatch Act"[3] for further guidance or contact the Office of the General Counsel.

In addition, nonpublic or sensitive information, personally identifiable information, and classified information may not be disclosed on public social media platforms.

> **Manager Alert**
>
> Personally identifiable or classified information may not be disclosed on public social media platforms.

GUIDELINES FOR USE OF SOCIAL MEDIA PLATFORMS

A variety of social media platforms are available to government managers and employees, including blogs, discussion forums, Facebook, Twitter, video and photo-sharing websites, and Wikipedia. Government managers and employees should be familiar with the federal guidelines for their use.

Blogs

Blog is Internet slang for *web log*. In its simplest form, a blog is simply a diary or journal stored on the Internet. It combines the global reach and informational value of a conventional site with the conversational exchanges of email. A typical blog combines text, images, and links to other blogs, web pages, and other media related to its topic.

Blogs can put a human face on government, as they are typically written informally. They can make government more "open" by enabling interaction between government and its citizens. Because material can be immediately posted, blogs allow agencies to respond quickly when they need to get information out quickly. A key component of blogging is that people can post comments and others can then comment on those comments. Additionally, blogs can be syndicated with RSS feeds (a web feed format used to publish frequently updated works), which propagate information to many media outlets.

> **Manager Alert**
>
> Blogs make government more "open" by enabling interaction between government and its citizens.

The General Services Administration (GSA) provides the following guidance for bloggers[4]:

- Blogs succeed when visitors feel they have reached a trusted source of information. Let readers know who the blogger is from a professional standpoint. Do not release any personal information that the general public should not know (for example, a home address or phone number).

- Be prepared to post content on a regular basis. This may mean daily or weekly, but not less frequently than every two weeks. Let readers know what the posting schedule is. Be realistic in preparing a schedule. It is always better to increase frequency over the life of a blog. If a blog remains idle for 60 days or more, GSA reserves the right to take it offline.
- Be prepared to make time and devote resources to moderating all comments that readers post. Be committed to read every comment received, even if nothing is posted in response to it. Time may be needed to research responses. Communicate to the audience the time frame within which the comment may be posted.
- Invite guest contributors. This is a great way to enhance value without increasing workload. Announce in advance who the guest contributors will be.
- Be prepared to respond on the blog to the posted comments, especially negative ones. Blogs build credibility and readership when they are as open as possible.
- If the same questions are posed over and over again, consider creating boilerplate responses to the questions.
- A blog should adhere to GSA Order, *GSA Logo and Visual System* (CSC 1808.1), which states, "the GSA Star Mark...will be used on all stationery, business cards, print and electronic communications products throughout the agency."
- Be aware that there are a variety of ways people will find the blog (e.g., via search engines, search and other e-mail alerts, RSS feeds, various social networking sites, book marking sites, e-mail from another person). This means that individuals will often read only a headline (or title) or a headline and a couple of sentences. The more intriguing and relevant the headline of the blog and the content that follows, the more likely the content is to build readership.

Although blogs can be valuable sources of news, information, and insights, not all comments are helpful or appropriate. Agencies routinely review comments and remove those that violate guidelines.

The U.S. Air Force offers the following guidelines for blogging:

- No classified information.
- Replace error with fact, not argument.
- Admit mistakes as soon as possible.
- Use your best judgment.
- Avoid the offensive, including defamatory, libelous, vulgar, obscene, abusive, profane, threatening, racially and ethnically hateful, or otherwise offensive or illegal information or material.

- Do not use material protected by copyright without the permission of the copyright owner. Consider using a Creative Commons license to protect your own work (free from creative-commons.org).
- Do not use trademarks without the permission of owners.
- Do not post material that would violate the proprietary, privacy, or personal rights of others.
- Avoid endorsements.
- No impersonations.
- Use disclaimers to let readers of a social media site or post know that the views you express are yours alone and do not reflect the views of the Air Force.
- Do not discuss areas of expertise for which you have no background or knowledge.
- You may provide a link from your site to an Air Force website.

In addition, guidelines from other agencies prohibit content that:

- Supports or opposes political campaigns or ballot measures
- Promotes, fosters, or perpetuates discrimination on the basis of race, creed, color, age, religion, gender, marital status, status with regard to public assistance, national origin, physical or mental disability, or sexual orientation
- Includes sexual content or links to sexual content
- Includes spam or comments obviously unrelated to the particular blog article.

These guidelines generally apply to any form of social media.

Discussion Forums

A discussion forum, or message board, is an online site where people can hold conversations in the form of posted messages. Discussion forums differ from chat rooms in that messages are at least temporarily archived. Unlike blogs, forums are created expressly to generate discussion or solicit opinions on a specific topic.

Depending on the access level of a user or the forum set-up, a posted message might need to be approved by a moderator before it becomes visible. A discussion forum is hierarchical or tree-like in structure; it can contain a number of subforums, each of which may have several topics. Within a forum's topic, each new discussion started is called a "thread," which can be replied to by any participant.

Depending on the forum's settings, users can be anonymous or they may have to register with the forum and then subsequently log in to post messages. On most forums, users do not have to log in to read existing messages.

Agencies vary in their policies and guidelines for discussion forums. The Environmental Protection Agency (EPA) requires approval from the Office of Public

Information and the Office of General Counsel (OGC) before a discussion forum may be set up. EPA and OGC consider answers to the following questions in their review:[5]

- What is the purpose and description of your discussion forum?
- Is your discussion forum related to a specific rulemaking? If so:
    - What rulemaking does it relate to?
    - How is the discussion related to the rulemaking?
    - At what stage of the rulemaking will the discussion forum be used? (preproposal, postproposal)
- What is the goal for your discussion forum?
- How does it serve the agency mission and your program goals?
- Who is your specific audience? Who will you reach out to for participation?
- Will you work with other programs, regions, federal agencies, or other partners to develop content?
- What is your communication strategy?
- Do you have the resources to create the content, promote this project, moderate the responses, and respond to questions and problems presented by your discussion forum?
- Will you participate in the discussion (engaging with responders)?
- What do you propose to name your discussion forum?
- When do you propose to launch it? How long will it be open for discussion? Are there events or dates that your discussion forum should be part of?

Facebook

Facebook is a social networking service with over one billion active users, more than half of whom access the site on a mobile device. Users must register to use Facebook, after which they may create a personal profile, add other users as friends, and exchange messages, including automatic notifications when they update their profile.[6]

Facebook provides government agencies with a platform for posting announcements, requesting feedback, asking questions, linking with an interested community, and providing both employees and citizens a place to share information. Government agencies, as well as other organizations, use "pages" instead of profiles. These pages can include an overview of a project, press releases, website and contact information, videos and photos, and RSS feeds from news releases, blogs, and the like.

When setting up a Facebook page, government managers should take care to

- Follow their agency's approval process

- Understand the steps involved in creating a page
- Follow guidelines for publishing, promoting, and managing a page
- Comply with Section 508 and other policies on accessibility, privacy, and recordkeeping
- Deal with fan posts and comments, especially those not meeting the guidelines for comments
- Track metrics to assess the effectiveness of a page, determine when and how to change the page, and decide if the investment is justified
- Avoid security risks.

EPA offers the following tips on managing a Facebook page:[7]

- Be both strategic and tactical. Plan your content to coincide with other outreach, but also post when you have something to say.
- Post updates weekly or more frequently. Share links, photos, videos, and other information. It's best to provide links to EPA's website with each update; if appropriate, also link to other sites per normal external link procedures.
- Use informal language, contractions, and first-person pronouns, and write as if you're talking to a friend, not writing a news release. For example:
    - No: *"EPA announces new program to provide benefits to ...."*
    - Yes: *"Hey, sign up to get benefits! We just started a new program."*
    - No: *"EPA will be providing individuals with ...."*
    - Yes: *"We'll give you ...."*
- Encourage discussion among fans by asking questions. Make sure the questions are open-ended to avoid Paperwork Reduction Act concerns.
- Ask for your community's thoughts, experiences, and stories.
- Listen to what commenters are saying and respond as appropriate. For more guidance on how to respond, please refer to the "Should I Respond Online on EPA's Behalf?" flowchart.[8]
- Start discussions using the "discussion" area of your page.
- Embed additional content, such as applications, widgets, and RSS feeds.
- Search Facebook for related pages and add them to your page's favorites, as appropriate. Post to their walls, and advertise your page there from time to time.

Twitter

Twitter is an example of a micro-blog, a real-time information network used by millions of individuals, organizations, and businesses to share information, commentary, and descriptions of events, as well as to highlight online and social media content. Twitter enables users to send and read messages made up of

140 characters or less, called "tweets." Tweets can be posted to Twitter via text message, mobile websites, audio, Twitter's website, or a variety of other mobile and web applications. When followers "retweet," or repeat a tweet, the message has the potential to spread far beyond the original followers. Twitter has an estimated 200 million users who generate more than 200 million tweets a day.[9]

EPA provides the following "rules for engagement" when using Twitter:

- Have a plan for the sort of content you will post: Is it an automated feed? Will you manually tweet to supplement automated content? Will you tweet manually only?
- The 140-character limit forces us to be pithy, clear, and catchy. Have some fun and be personable with phrasing, but always in good taste. If in doubt whether your words may cross the line, ask a colleague for a second opinion.
- Try to stay at least 10–20 characters below the 140-character limit. This facilitates retweeting, which requires enough characters beyond the original tweet to include your "@username" (plus "RT" and a space, if they are manually retweeting you). It also allows for comment. Think "120 is the new 140."
- Tweet at least daily.
- Content is king: Provide information, insight, and clarification.
- Don't procrastinate about whether to tweet. Timeliness matters.
- Respond to questions, but stick to your area of expertise. People might ask you questions you can't answer; refer them to someone who can.
- Respond to complaints if you can help someone, but avoid arguing with people trying to bait you (referred to as "trolls" on the Internet).
- Reply and retweet. The more you engage, the more people will respect you.
- Solicit tweet suggestions from others in your office who are knowledgeable about your subject.
- Phrase questions so that they are open-ended; ask for thoughts or ideas.
- Link to more in-depth content, such as a webpage, podcast, or news release. Use a URL shortener like bit.ly to keep the length down. Use GSA's go.usa.gov shortener for .gov links.
- Cover only one point and provide only one link per tweet. To direct people to more comprehensive information, link to a page that then links to multiple pages.
- Keep automatic posts to a minimum, but in some cases, fully automated accounts are valuable. Use twitterfeed.com to establish those posts. Mention automation in your bio to tell people what to expect.

- Tag topics of ongoing interest using a hashtag to allow for easy searching (e.g., #opengov). Use the same hashtag on all tweets related to specific outreach campaigns.
- Check your spelling. You can't correct errors. You can delete a given post, but it will still appear in searches.

Don't:

- Tweet about things you wouldn't talk about under other circumstances. As with email, if you don't want to see it on the front page of the newspaper, don't tweet it.
- Lobby, promote political viewpoints, or endorse commercial products.
- Argue, push personal opinions, or get into long-running debates.
- Let your account languish.

Manager Alert

One valuable social media resource for managers is GovLoop, an externally hosted social network catering to federal employees. GovLoop has hundreds of groups, one of which is the Professional Managers Association, an organization that serves as a voice of managers in the federal government. Check it out at www.govloop.com/group/professional-managers-association.

Video and Photo-Sharing Websites

Online video and photo-sharing websites, such as YouTube, Flickr, SmugMug, and Snapfish, are popular and powerful media for exchanging information. Using these sites, anyone with Internet access can upload, share, view, and comment on photos or video footage. The process of sharing videos among individuals and groups is sometimes called "viral video sharing."

YouTube has emerged as one of the Internet's most popular websites. More than 20 hours of video files are uploaded to the site every minute and 50 percent of users view videos online at least weekly.[10]

The Center for Disease Control (CDC) provides the following guidelines for developing videos specifically for dissemination on YouTube:[11]

- Clearly define your objectives. It is important to have clearly defined objectives before beginning to develop your video. Do you want to highlight content, spark action, or encourage awareness of an issue? Clarify your objectives first and determine if a video on YouTube or other video-sharing site is the ideal channel for your message. A common objective for online video is viral sharing through peer-to-peer networks.

- Know your target audience. As with any communications activity, it is important to define your intended target audience to ensure that you develop and communicate messages and graphics that resonate with your audience and prompt them to take action. Tailoring messages and video content to match your target audience will aid the marketing and dissemination process.
- Review your content. All CDC.gov videos ready for posting online should not only contain cleared content, but should be engaging and visually pleasing, and should be presented at a level appropriate for the target audience. Avoid jargon, technical information, or detailed charts and graphs. Simple, easy-to-follow "stories" work best, with a single message or call to action.

Wikipedia

Wikipedia is a resource for conducting research as well as a community of people with similar interests who help shape and guide what is posted under entries online. The fundamental principles by which Wikipedia operates are summarized in its five "pillars." These pillars provide important guidelines for anyone wanting to either research or contribute to the website:[12]

- Wikipedia is an encyclopedia. It combines many features of general and specialized encyclopedias, almanacs, and gazetteers. Wikipedia is not a soapbox, an advertising platform, a vanity press, an experiment in anarchy or democracy, an indiscriminate collection of information, or a web directory. It is not a dictionary, a newspaper, or a collection of source documents, although some of its fellow Wikimedia projects are.
- Wikipedia is written from a neutral point of view. We strive for articles that document and explain the major points of view in a balanced and impartial manner. We avoid advocacy and we characterize information and issues rather than debate them. In some areas there may be just one well-recognized point of view; in others, we describe multiple points of view, presenting each accurately and in context rather than as "the truth" or "the best view." All articles must strive for verifiable accuracy, citing reliable, authoritative sources, especially when the topic is controversial or a living person. Editors' personal experiences, interpretations, or opinions do not belong.
- Wikipedia is free content that anyone can edit, use, modify, and distribute. All editors freely license their work to the public; no editor owns an article and any contributions can and will be mercilessly edited and redistributed. Respect copyright laws, and never plagiarize from sources. Borrowing non-free media is sometimes allowed as fair use, but strive to find free alternatives first.
- Editors should interact with each other in a respectful and civil manner. Respect your fellow Wikipedians, even when you disagree. Apply Wikipedia etiquette, and avoid personal attacks. Seek consensus, avoid edit wars, and never disrupt Wikipedia to illustrate a point. Act in good faith, and assume good faith on the

part of others. Be open and welcoming. If a conflict arises, discuss it calmly on the nearest talk pages, follow dispute resolution procedures, and remember that there are 4,163,602 other articles on the English Wikipedia to work on and discuss.

- Wikipedia does not have firm rules. Wikipedia has policies and guidelines, but they are not carved in stone; their content and interpretation can evolve over time. Their principles and spirit matter more than their literal wording, and sometimes improving Wikipedia requires making an exception. Be bold, but not reckless, in updating articles and do not agonize about making mistakes. Every past version of a page is saved, so any mistakes can be easily corrected.

SECURITY RISKS AND MITIGATION STRATEGIES

Federal government information systems are targeted by persistent, pervasive, aggressive threats. To defend against rapidly evolving social media threats, federal departments and agencies should incorporate a multilayered approach in a risk management program, including risks to the individual, risks to the department or agency, and risks to the federal infrastructure. The Chief Information Officer's (CIO) "Guidelines for Secure Use of Social Media by Federal Departments and Agencies"[13] provides guidance for any federal agency that uses social media services to collaborate and communicate among employees, partners, other federal agencies, and the public.

The following is an abbreviated description of risks and mitigation strategies from the CIO guidelines.

Types of Risks

Social media technologies such as wikis, blogs, and social networks are vulnerable to three types of cyber attacks:

- *Spear phishing* is an attack targeting a specific user or group of users that attempts to deceive the user into performing an action that launches an attack, such as opening a document or clicking a link. Spear phishers rely on knowing some personal piece of information about their target, such as an event, interest, travel plans, or current issues. Participants in social media should be careful in clicking on links and communicating with other members of online groups.
- *Social engineering* relies on exploiting the human element of trust. The first step in any social engineering attack is to collect information about the attacker's target. Social networking websites can reveal a large amount of personal information, including resumes, home addresses, phone numbers, employment information, work locations, family members, education, photos,

and private information. Social media websites may share more personal information than users expect or need to keep in touch.

- *Web application attacks* are dynamic web pages that use scripting to provide additional functionality to the user. Social media websites are advanced web applications, and this opens them up to a wide range of vulnerabilities exploitable by attackers. Advances in web application technologies allow attackers to use new techniques against social media websites not previously possible in email.

Strategies for Minimizing Risk

The risks involved are serious, but they should not be a reason or an excuse not to use social media. While launching attacks like these is technically complex, all you need to avoid them is a little bit of knowledge and common sense. The following are some strategies federal managers can use to minimize risk and use social media safely:

- *Procedural controls.* The most important question in ensuring the safe use of social media tools is not "what tools do we use?" but "how do we use them?" Any use of social media should be accompanied by some thoughtful operating procedures. Be explicit about the type of data or information you will share. Who is authorized to post content? Who is authorized to approve it? Prepare a brief document that captures your goals and objectives for use of social media, including what types of interactions you are and are not seeking to engage in. Create operating procedures for content filtering and monitoring to address functional areas of system administration and user behavior, including limiting specific activities or disallowing certain traffic (such as third-party applications).
- *Acquisition controls.* Most social media services provide administrative features that can customize how information is collected from and provided to the public, either bundled with the service or for an additional fee. Consider comparing the feature sets of platforms side by side, or engaging vendors to inquire about the security and privacy features they provide. Consider whether platforms that use voting or public comment are prone to being "gamed" or invite cheating or fraud, and what measures can be taken to prevent it.
- *Training controls.* The key to using social media securely is ensuring that everyone who uses it has access to sufficient training materials and opportunities. Periodic awareness and training campaigns can help educate users about what information to share, with whom they can share it, and what not to share. Employees should also be trained to protect not to blur their personal and professional lives, and should be provided guidance on whether and how they should identify themselves on social media websites, depending on their official role.

> **Manager Alert**
>
> For more information on government social media, go to www.howto.gov/social-media/using-social-media.

NOTES

1. www.opm.gov/news/social-media-presence/social-media-policy.pdf (accessed February 2013).
2. For a full discussion of OPM's social media policy, see www.opm.gov/news/social-media-presence/social-media-policy.pdf (accessed February 2013).
3. www.osc.gov/documents/hatchact/federal/Social%20Media%20and%20the%20Hatch%20Act%202012.pdf (accessed February 2013).
4. *The Social Media Navigator: GSA's Guide to Official Use of Social Media*, www.gsa.gov/graphics/staffoffices/socialmedianavigator.pdf (accessed February 2013).
5. http://govsocmed.pbworks.com/w/page/27519826/EPA%20Social%20Media%20Guidance%20Documents (accessed February 2013).
6. http://en.wikipedia.org/wiki/Facebook (accessed February 2013).
7. http://govsocmed.pbworks.com/w/page/27521304/EPA%20Facebook%20Guidance (accessed February 2013).
8. http://www.epa.gov/irmpoli8/policies/respond.pdf (accessed February 2013).
9. www.cdc.gov/socialmedia/tools/guidelines/pdf/twitterguidelines.pdf (accessed February 2013).
10. www.youtube.com/t/fact_sheet (accessed February 2013).
11. www.cdc.gov/socialmedia/tools/guidelines/pdf/onlinevideo.pdf (accessed February 2013).
12. http://en.wikipedia.org/wiki/Wikipedia:Five_pillars (accessed February 2013).
13. https://cio.gov/wp-content/uploads/downloads/2012/09/Guidelines_for_Secure_Use_Social_Media_v01-0.pdf (accessed February 2013).

INDEX